Buying and Selling
A Home in Ireland:
Need to Know Guide

Buying and Selling A Home Ireland:
Need to Know Guide

Damian McHugh, B.L.

Published in 2005
by First Law Limited
Merchant's Court
Merchants Quay
Dublin 8
Ireland
www.firstlaw.ie

This book was typeset by Artwerk Ltd., Dublin
and printed by Judita Press, Dublin.

© First Law Limited

ISBN 1-904480-27-6

A catalogue record for this book
is available from the British Library.

This book is dedicated to the memory of the late
Martin (Marty) Howley

FOREWORD

It goes without saying that the greatest personal purchase and/or sale of your life will not be achieved without a very considerable input of research, patience, time and the outlay of a frighteningly high amount of borrowed money.

The majority of consumers approach property sales and purchases with limits in their confidence, in their ability to actively participate and in every facet of cost incurred. They must commence dealings with a variety of property professionals and other agents who will assist them through the process. This requires that they put their trust in others and their hands, regularly, into their pocket in payment for those services. Therefore, it makes essential sense that this time and money be well spent.

Now, here in his third guide, *Buying and Selling A Home in Ireland: Need to Know Guide*, Damian McHugh provides every consumer, buyer, seller, builder and investor with the route, the tools and the means of getting through it all. The reader quickly learns that property dealing may be bigger and require you to interact with a multitude of service providers but that, with the assistance of this excellent book, you can exercise a strong degree of control. Control which should see you through because it empowers the reader to confront the realities, ask all of the hard questions and leave vulnerability behind.

As Damian quite correctly indicates from the outset, the property landscape in Ireland and across the EU is changing. There are recommendations for legal, environmental and financial change and significant high level ongoing reviews of our own regulatory and planning provisions. With so much movement and change in the property market the requirement that the buyer and seller beware holds a stronger emphasis than it ever did.

You are going to be dealing with solicitors, finance houses, estate agents, insurance companies, removal companies, property managers, planning officials and a whole array of other agents on whom you will rely. What must be remembered is that you rely on them because you are dealing with buyers and sellers and it is they who are, arguably, the most unreliable actors throughout the entire process.

When the dust, literally, has settled and you look back you will realise that preparation is half the battle and, in the purchase or sale of your property, this was the best handbook any soldier could buy!

**Dermott Jewell,
Chief Executive,
Consumers' Association of Ireland.**

PREFACE

This is a book about the law, or more especially a process, involving aspects of many different laws that effect or impinge on everybody, in either buying or in selling a residential property. It is an attempt at drawing together and simplifying for consumers what is involved in this very expensive process that results in the sale or purchase of a house or apartment. In a way, it goes behind the façade of such transactions to shed some light on the very many legal and procedural strands that are fused together in buying or selling a residential property. It is not exhaustive but, hopefully, is a fairly comprehensive effort at explaining the very many steps that lead to an individual or a couple buying or selling their home.

Law and the practice of law continues to evolve and change. Many aspects of law are involved in the sale and purchase of houses and apartments. These include the law of land, contract law, conveyancing, landlord and tenant and family, each of which is substantive in its own right. Latterly, it is involving European Union law more and more, as illustrated in chapter 11, which deals with the energy performance of buildings, including houses and apartments. An individual or couple buying a house today in one of the many new developments throughout Ireland, will someday have to provide a certificate of energy performance related to their heating system if they decide to sell. The property they are selling will have to comply with certain minimum standards. While the nuts and bolts of this are being worked out in the Department of the Environment at the moment, the fact is that it had its origins in Brussels and Strasbourg where the EU Council and Parliament, respectively introduced the new law, in the form of a Directive which member states are obliged to transpose into their own domestic law. In fact, the signature of the then president of the parliament, Ireland's Pat Cox is on the Directive. Some day also, because of other EU developments currently under consideration, people buying homes and apartments in Ireland may be able to buy their mortgage from a German-based lender, or in an English bank or building society or in some other EU member state which will offer better rates than those available in Ireland. The idea behind this initiative is to rationalise mortgages and other services for the benefit of consumers.

The landscape is changing, not just for the buyers and sellers of residential property, but also for the service providers, the banks, the buildings societies who may be jointly termed, lenders, and for the professionals who effect the change in ownership of houses and apartments for consumers, the lawyers.

Putting the finishing touches to this book has coincided with publication of the long-awaited report of the Competition Authority into the legal profession. It contains many proposals which, if implemented, would change the face of legal practice in this country. It looks closely at the supply of conveyancing services and notes that under section 58 of the Solicitors Act 1954 only solicitors could provide those services to the public for payment. One of its proposals is for the introduction of legislation permitting financial institutions to provide conveyancing services to the public 'by way of employed solicitors or other qualified persons.' The purpose of this book is to guide the steps of buyers and sellers of residential property in a general way and to advise them on the basis of the law and conveyancing procedures as they are, not as they might be. Therefore, it will not get involved in the merits or otherwise of the Authority's proposals. Whether lenders are permitted to open 'one-stop shops' in terms of providing mortgages, insurance and legal services, or whether conveyancing is opened up to barristers or other 'licensed conveyancers,' is a matter for others and not for discussion here. The only reason it is mentioned is to illustrate yet a further development that impinges on the business of buying and selling residential property, which continues to be vibrant.

The important thing is that consumers, the ordinary men and women in Ireland, are able to buy and sell houses and apartments as efficiently and as reasonably as possible and, in addition, are fully protected by their own, exclusive legal adviser, working totally independent of a lender or any other party with a vested interest. People buying a house or an apartment are not interested in the politics or discussion opened up by what is only a preliminary report. They need value for money and as much guidance as possible. Hopefully, this book will go some way in doing just that, by generally directing their steps in the right direction.

It is some years since one had to go through the legal texts but, thankfully, many of the most valuable were to hand for easy reference, including J.C.W. Wylie's *Irish Land Law* and *Irish Conveyancing Law*, and also the Law Society's *Conveyancing*, all of which were most helpful, not only in refreshing my memory but in up-dating me in many ways for the benefit of readers. My sincere thanks are due to a number of solicitors for their guidance, including Paul O'Brien, Robert Pierse (Listowel, Co. Kerry), Deborah McHugh and Dearbhla Considine. I received great assistance from Robert McHugh, valuation surveyor, and Lyndsey Blackmore of the Planning Department, Wicklow County Council. Nancy Callaghan, of the building standards section at the Department of the Environment, Heritage and Local Government and her colleagues in the Housing section, were equally generous in furnishing me with information, as was Sonja O'Gorman of Sherry Fitzgerald O'Gorman, and not forgetting Cathal Cooney, Chartered Accountant, who opened up the word of financial services to me. My thanks also to Thérèse Carrick for editing the manuscript. This is the third book that I have been commissioned to write by Bart Daly, Managing Director of the publishers, First Law Ltd, all for the benefit of the public, colloquially described for the purposes of each book as 'consumers.' He deserves the plaudits for identifying the particular areas that the books – the others being *Going to Court: A Consumer's Guide* and *Small Claims Court in Ireland: A Consumer's Guide* - should be focussed on. If *Buying and Selling A Home: Need to Know Guide* succeeds in cutting through the tangled web of the conveyancing process and helps to inform buyers in that process, it will have achieved its objective. Last, but not least, I want to express sincere appreciation to my wife, Claire, and our children, for their forbearance and patience during the long periods that I was closeted working away on this task.

Damian McHugh
April 2005

Table of Contents

TABLE OF LEGISLATION

Chapter 1

PRELIMINARY STEPS IN BUYING AND SELLING

Most people know when they have found the home they have been looking for. The moment of decision may well have come out of the blue. It could have followed weeks, months or even years of mental, financial or other preparation or, perhaps a combination of these. It may even have been a decision made on the spur of the moment. Whatever the lead up, the decision to buy a particular premises may be accompanied by a feeling of elation. Most especially this occurs when buying a first home. The 'cloud nine' feeling may soon be tempered with thoughts of fear or even dread as the realisation of the huge financial step that has been embarked on begins to sink in. Whatever else it may be, this is a moment for a cool head.

Potential buyers of houses and apartments are virtually inundated in today's market with colourful advertisements in daily, evening and even Sunday newspapers, on radio and television commercials, announcing the launch of new houses and apartments. Some offer incentives to woo the prospective buyers. Such saturation coverage, albeit at a cost to the developer/seller, is designed to present the respective development in the most attractive state. The language is usually colourful and inviting.

In some places, sales offices have been reinvented. They are now called marketing suites which are usually custom-built on site with flags flying proudly outside. They are adorned inside with expensive glossy brochures and site maps, showing off the benefits of living in the particular area. Eager sales staff are on hand to answer every question. Everything is positive and simple. It is only a matter of paying a deposit and having a coloured pin stuck on a house or apartment in the map on the wall. The house or apartment is yours. It is done and dusted. Right? Not really. It is only the beginning of a long and somewhat tortuous procedure that, hopefully, culminates in the buyer walking in the front door and thinking, 'A home of my own at last.'

On the other hand, when a person decides **to sell their home**, they should do their utmost to present the property in the best light possible in order to attract potential buyers, without going to extremes. Views may differ between estate agents as to what should be done by the seller before putting the property on the market. Some might advise re-tiling a floor or, perhaps, replacing carpet with wooden floors. Others might say that it would not warrant such expenditure and trouble. Whatever the right answer, it is a subjective question in each individual sale. However, touching up a room with more modern colours and a general clean-up and possibly 'make-over' may pay dividends in attracting genuine potential purchasers, as distinct from 'curtain pullers' solely interested in viewing the furniture and décor during a regular reconnaissance of properties for sale, new and second-hand. This is a good reason to employ a vigilant estate agent who can recognise the genuine buyer when they sign in to view a property.

CAUTION

In the midst of the euphoria of finding a new or second-hand house must come common sense and the adage favoured by a wise acquaintance: 'Think twice and hammer once,' or the doctor friend who had this sign on his desk 'think twice, then prescribe.' Applied to this particular situation it means a person must think twice before taking the all-important step of actually buying. **You buy to sell** You must buy a residential unit, which you will be able to sell, if and when you decide to sell and possibly trade-up. Whether you buy off the plans in the cosy atmosphere of a showhouse or apartment especially fitted out with the most modern furniture and appliances, fixtures and fittings that a commissioned designer can produce or has been reproduced by sales staff from the pages of a better homes' magazine, or in a normal private treaty situation or at auction, extreme caution is advised.

Potential buyers can be vulnerable in the face of such sales and marketing techniques
They must be aware of the fact that the advice and help of many professionals employed by the developer have gone into the preparation of the house or apartment for presentation to the public. If buyers feel they have been coerced into buying, they should not hesitate to ask for their deposit to be returned.

BOOKING DEPOSIT
It is time to slow down, to step back and ponder what will happen if the booking deposit cheque is handed over. Can the money be recovered if the buyer has a mind change? Should the house or apartment be surveyed before any money is paid down or, at least, before contracts are exchanged? Should a solicitor be engaged immediately?

MORTGAGE
Because of the enormous financial considerations involved in the purchase of property today, is it prudent to seek loan approval from a bank or building society, before or after a booking deposit is paid?

CHOOSING A SOLICITOR
What exactly will the chosen legal adviser be doing for the fee or, for that matter, how does one go about choosing a solicitor who will protect the interests of the buyer? The same considerations apply to a seller in choosing a solicitor to handle the sale. These are just some of the many issues that must be addressed, very early on, in order to feel comfortable with the whole process being undertaken. At this preliminary stage, the advice is to shop around as the amount of legal professional fees for conveyancing transactions can vary widely.

COUPLES

If the house or apartment is being purchased by two people who are unmarried -in a strict legal sense - different considerations will apply. Should they buy jointly or in common? What, legally, does 'jointly' mean or, for that matter, what does 'in common' mean in this context? Should there be a contract in such circumstances which would provide a 'let-out' or exit strategy should either of the parties wish to leave the property or sell their interest in the property or buy out the other partner? What would be the legal and practical consequences of putting their names jointly or in common on the title deeds? The partners might be two brothers or two sisters, or a brother and sister, or just two friends who wish to enter the property market. In the case of cohabitees, what would happen the property if they should remain unmarried but their personal relationship ended and they went their separate ways? These are extremely important questions, which must be confronted by each individual before entering into such a serious commitment.

The same considerations apply if a house, for example, were purchased for habitation by two couples. What legal issues would arise if, at some stage, they decide to go their separate ways? If this contingency had not been adverted to when the contract was being drawn up, it would have legal and financial implications for the parties. We will return to some of these issues in chapter 12.

GUIDELINES

However, first things first. Presuming that the house-hunting is only beginning, very serious thought must be given to what type of property is being sought, its probable location and, most of all, the cost. The questions uppermost should be:-

- Should the property be located in the city, town, village or countryside; rural versus urban living. Both have advantages and disadvantages that are all too obvious to anybody who has lived in either. The decision is very important in terms of not only cost and environment, but also health. While property is less expensive outside urban areas, so also is house and car insurance. However, while there are undoubted benefits living in the countryside, there are downsides to this. The smells that emanate from a farmer's field may be too strong to bear for many people who don't have a rural background. While some people moving into this kind of life-style will find their social life may be limited, others will indulge themselves in a small community and get involved in sporting and community affairs. In fact, the social life - other than the pub - that can be all too rare in urban living may only begin once the move to a rural way of life is made. There is also the option of a semi-rural location such as on the outskirts of a town or village scattered the length and breath of Ireland.

- Seclusion from neighbours and distance from shops and other facilities can be important factors, especially for parents with children. The family car may become a taxi, ferrying children back and forth to schools, to the houses of friends, into towns and cities to discos, cinemas and other places of entertainment. Perhaps, because of the pressure on the family car, a second car, with attendant costs, may be needed. An idyllic dream may become a nightmare in reality.

- Is the property that you want as your home to be a house or apartment?

HOUSE INQUIRIES
- If it is to be a house, will it be new or old. The latter, although colloquially known as second-hand, may be very old and may have had many owners, each of whom would have put their own personal imprint on the house. Stamp duty is payable on second-hand residential

properties. It is not applicable in the case of some new houses; it is payable on other new houses in certain circumstances. Given the cost of houses generally, the applicable rate of stamp duty can be considerable, as we will see, despite the most recent budgetary relief.

• If the house is to be located in a new housing scheme, how good or bad are the local services. Can public transport be relied on to get you to your place of work? Is the area well served with shops, restaurants and other facilities? If there are children whose education has to be considered, are there primary and secondary schools nearby. How good are they? Will it be possible to enrol a child or children in either? Are there other children of similar age to your own child or children in the neighbourhood?

• If you are considering a second-hand house, many of the same issues will need to be looked at. In addition, the house will need to be surveyed, but the cost of repairs, improvements, modernising and decorating will also be part of the pre-purchase checklist for the buyer. There is the added cost here of stamp duty, details of which we will look at later.

• Perhaps, the buyer might want to buy an old house to restore it before converting it into a comfortable home. But large, detached houses are expensive to heat, so thought must be given to the long-term reality of the costs associated with living in the completed house. In addition, there may be planning or other restrictions, such as listing, which prohibit or limit what can be done with the building. Therefore, pre-contract inquiries by your solicitor, will be an essential pre-requisite to establish what the true position is in this respect.

• What are the neighbours like? Things may not always be what they seem, and this may be as true of the property itself as it may be of the people who live nearby. A few inquiries may effect a change of mind... either way.

- Privacy and seclusion may be an important consideration for some. But so, too, may be a willingness for other people to become involved in busy community life.

- Is a garden necessary? A garden that needs constant attention may not be a priority for singles and also childless couples with busy work and social schedules.

- Is a garage or parking facilities needed?

- Will it be necessary to take somebody in as a tenant to help pay the mortgage? Therefore, is a second or even third bedroom an essential requirement?

- Will the property need special disabled access?

- Perhaps the buyer might need to consider whether to buy a site, with or without planning permission, and build a house to their own design. If this is the choice, location is again paramount. So also is cost and many of the other factors mentioned above. The water supply and sewage are very important considerations. Perhaps a septic tank will have to be installed, and a well drilled to try and find a fresh water supply. The future maintenance of these is also a consideration However, unlike buying a new or second-hand house or apartment, different considerations apply in financing such an undertaking. For example, the method of drawing down funds and paying the builder is different. It involves what is known as stage payments, meaning getting the money to pay the builder from the bank or building society when you need it at different stages of the construction. Bridging finance may also be necessary to cover a situation that could occur where you and your advisers underestimated the amount of the original loan or mortgage needed to buy and service the site and build the house. This is not unusual.

APARTMENTS

Statistics show that most people opt from flat or apartment ownership to house purchase. Unlike houses, which generally tend to be freehold today (a term that will be explained fully later), most apartments are leasehold (This, also, will be explained). Therefore, if, at the outset, an apartment is the preferred option, other considerations will apply. These include:-

- The cost of the **maintenance contract** that will be entered into at the same time and as a condition of purchase. On average, this service charge can range from an annual fee of about €1,000, together with another €200 for a garage space for a car, for a one-bedroom apartment to about €1400 or €1500 a year for a two-bedroom apartment and garage space. Service charges way in excess of these amounts are charged in some apartment developments, running into thousands of Euros. A phenomenon with new private housing developments in recent years is the advent of the maintenance contract also being signed up to when contracts are exchanged. Paying an annual service charge of hundreds of Euros becomes a term of the contract and legally binds the house buyer. Whatever it may be, it is a considerable outlay on top of mortgage payments and requires much consideration before the decision to buy is made.

- The fact that the owner will be subject to a management contract which debars the apartment owner from making structural changes to the property, such as building a balcony, without the approval of the management company. (The same considerations may apply to a person buying a residential property of a type known as a townhouse in a new housing scheme). One reason for this is that the apartment owner only owns the internal face of the walls of the apartment because of the fact that they are what are known as party walls.

- The conditions, rules or **covenants** in the contract also bind the owner tenant as to their behaviour while in occupation. For example, they cannot make noise, such as playing loud music, so as to interfere with the peaceful enjoyment and occupation of the other tenant owners. There are also covenants binding the management company, which is usually a representative of the company, which developed the apartments. The tenant owners will also be represented. The conditions or covenants are very similar to the covenants contained in a normal written lease for a residential property. The one big difference, of course, is the length of the lease. The long lease in respect of the new or old apartment being purchased will be, on average for 999 years.

- The location of the apartment is extremely important with view and a sunny aspect important considerations. Also its proximity to public transport, shops and other facilities.

FIRST DUTY FOR BUYERS AND SELLERS

At a very early stage in the process of actually deciding to **buy or sell** a home, the individual should first **register with one or more estate agents** operating in the area. A **seller** should approach an agent with a good track record in selling property, or similar property, in the same area in which the property is located. Sometimes, it might be prudent to get two agents to handle the sale, with the fees going to the agent who successfully finds the buyer for the property. However, advertising costs in this situation would obviously be higher.

A **buyer** will look for the housing or apartment lists from the various estate agents who have a presence in the area they are interested in. The agents readily provide information and brochures and will arrange inspections to suit both the potential buyer and the seller. If they have nothing that interests the buyer at a particular time, the buyer should ask to be put on their mailing list. In this way they will be kept informed when the agents have other properties on their books that might suit.

Buyers should be conscious of the fact that if an agent has a property for sale or auction, the agent will be exclusively representing the seller, not the buyer. Buyers can ask around and seek out an estate agent who will act solely for him/her. As with sellers, reputation and track record in a particular area should again influence buyers in deciding who to appoint.

THE INTERNET

With the popularity of Internet browsing and the availability of some excellent websites in Ireland offering information on houses and apartments for sale in most locations in the country, complete with illustrations and virtual tours in some cases, liberal use should be made of the computer. It is an invaluable tool in the sale of, and in the hunt for, property in Ireland today.

NEWSPAPERS

The property pages of newspapers remain one of the best sources of information but don't just rely on the large coloured advertisements. The house or apartment you are seeking may well be 'hidden' in a small classified advertisement in not just the daily, Sunday or weekly newspaper but in an evening newspaper. This is where the author and his wife found their first home in leafy Terenure, Dublin 6, many years ago. Therefore, every avenue should be explored in the quest of finding or selling a home.

Chapter 2

FINANCIAL AND OTHER ADVICE

TAKING THE BOLD STEP

The financial considerations addressed in this chapter relate mainly to **buyers,** who have to face up to the huge financial undertaking associated with the purchase of a new home and the building of their own home, from the very beginning. It is one thing to take out a chequebook and write a cheque for the deposit you have been scrimping and saving for over a long period; it is another thing to meet the heavy payments on an ongoing basis. Many people engage the services of a financial advisor at the outset and this is a good thing in itself. However, just as it is crucial to get a solicitor who works solely for you, the buyer, and not for you *and* the vendor or seller of the property at the same time, so also is it advisable for the buyer to shop around to seek the services of somebody who has their exclusive interests at heart. An independent **broke**r would fit into this category. However, while some brokers are 'tied' to certain building societies and insurers, many others are independent.

There is absolutely nothing wrong in taking advice from an adviser attached to a particular bank or building society. In fact, it should be encouraged. They are well informed and qualified to handle your business and, like all financial institutions and advisers, are monitored by the **Irish Financial Services Regulatory Authority (IFSRA)**. The more you shop around in the different institutions, the more information you will get about their particular financial packages, including the types of mortgage that are available, the different variable and fixed interest rates as well as a 'sweetener' for first-time buyers in the form of discounted interest rates, during the first 12 months usually. However, there are a number of caveats to taking advice from these institutions:

- They are in the business of making a profit and they will try and talk you into buying one of their products which may, or may not, offer a lower rate of interest on the loan or mortgage than a similar product from a competitor. Given that it may take up to 35 years to pay off the mortgage, and that you may be paying even a small fraction of a percent higher than the rate available from another lender, a slightly higher interest rate will add thousands of Euros to your bill during the life of the mortgage.

- Money is plentiful and readily available to qualifying buyers in Ireland today. It wasn't always so. There was a time when a person would painstakingly complete a mortgage application form of several pages, submit the necessary certificate of earnings (possibly boosted artificially with the addition of overtime and bonuses payments masquerading as basic pay) and wait on 'tender hooks' for a number of weeks before getting the welcome letter of approval from the bank or building society. It certainly was an occasion of great joy. Money was scarce and many applications might have to be submitted to different financial institutions before success was achieved. One particular building society was better than others at giving mortgage approvals. However, the price for this was that borrowers were paying anything from one-quarter to 1% above the going rate for this 'privilege.' Nobody minded. They now had their own home but at a higher cost. Thankfully, times have changed for the better and there is stiff competition for business among the credit organisations and financial institutions operating in the Irish market.

- Individual financial institutions may try and sell a product, such as an **endowment mortgage**, which should only be bought after taking the most serious independent financial, and possibly legal, advice. These have become notorious, not just in England where it has assumed national prominence, but here in Ireland in the last couple of years. It is a type of mortgage where the mortgage interest is paid each month and the capital is repaid from the proceeds of an endowment policy with an insurance company. The author has personal experience of this. It was some years after we entered into such a mortgage arrangement that it became apparent that there was a big question mark over whether the proceeds of the insurance policy would be sufficient to pay off in full the amount of the mortgage that had been advanced. Instead of receiving a lump sum of money at maturity - which was the basis on which the product was 'sold' to us by our bank - shortfalls have become the order of the day. Imagine the shock the householder would receive when, instead of getting a welcome boost of money, the institution would, instead, be demanding payment of several thousand Euro. No such risk was advanced by the particular institution in selling the endowment mortgage to the author who, again, was naive to the fact that the financial institution 'agent' was earning personal commission from the insurance company his institution was tied with. When the risk of a possible underpayment become apparent after receiving advice from an independent expert, an ordinary variable mortgage from a different financial institution was obtained to pay off the original lender. Legal fees of about IR£300 were incurred as a result, but that was a small price to pay for knowing that the house would be paid for when the time came to redeem (pay-off) the mortgage.

- There was a time when it was impossible to change or switch from one lender to another, even though the financial institution a person had their mortgage with, was charging an interest rate considerably higher than a competitor. Today, it is not only possible to switch but people are encouraged to switch. There would be a saving in mortgage repayments but whether the transfer is worth the outlay in terms of the legal fees charged by your solicitor for effecting the transfer or switch, depends very much on the number of years the mortgage has to run. At least one bank and an online finance intermediary offered to **switch mortgages without incurring legal fees** earlier this year. If a person is considering a switch, they should shop around for the best deal, not only in terms of lower interest rates but the legal fees that may be incurred as a result.

- Be conscious of the fact that advisers who work in banks and building societies are not independent. They will recommend their own products and also those of an insurance company they are 'tied' to. Again, it must be emphasised that there is nothing legally wrong with such an arrangement or of dealing with these advisers.

- Sometimes a bank or building society which financed, or partly financed, the construction of a scheme of houses or apartments has a representative in the showhouse or apartment, or in a sales or marketing suite, trying to sign up the new buyers. This site presence is obviously pre-arranged with the developer as a *quid pro quo* for providing finance for the construction of the new houses or apartments. Buyers are free to talk with the representative, of course, but they would be advised not to enter into any firm commitment, especially at this early stage when they may not have shopped around and they might be vulnerable and unprepared to deal with the long-term effect of entering into an arrangement for a particular type of mortgage.

- Buyers need all the advice they can get from as wide a variety of sources as possible. This will enable them to make an informed choice in the final analysis.

- In seeking out an independent adviser, buyers have several options. They can get independent advice through the offices of a **chartered accountant**, who may have a financial services brokerage as part of or in conjunction with the practice. There are also other independents operating in the market. Some are 'tied' agents of certain banks, building societies and insurance companies. Others are not. Some will charge for their services, while others will not. Those who do not charge, will receive their remuneration from the financial institution or insurance company they introduce the buyer and his/her business to. However, all are qualified to offer their services under the Investment Intermediaries Act 1995, having studied and passed examinations in order to be able to do so.

- Don't be rushed into making a decision just because you are offered loan approval very quickly. It is a buyer's market at present and has been so for a considerable time. The financial institutions know that. The fact is that most lenders can offer loan approval almost instantly. However, in this rush, a person might feel they have been coerced, even to a small degree, into signing up and paying a deposit, If they do, they should not hesitate subsequently to ask for their deposit back. Should this or similar problem between a buyer and the financial institution and insurers which provided the mortgage and insurance, respectively, remain unresolved, rather than going to law over the matter the buyer could refer it to the **Financial Services Ombudsman** who investigates complaints from customers of regulated financial service providers.

In the next chapter we will look at the expense related to the fact of having to pay service charges, whether you will be living in an apartment or, indeed, in one of the new private housing estates. They have become part and parcel of the contract to purchase a residential unit in one of these developments but what does a person get for their money, which can range from €400 or €500 a year to several thousands of Euros, depending on the type of property and its location? It would include:

- The maintenance of lifts.

- The cleaning of the common areas, such as corridors in apartment blocks.

- Garbage disposal in apartments, but not in housing developments.

- Pest control.

- Payments of a maintenance person's or caretaker's salary.

- Buildings insurance in the case of apartments and third party liability insurance in the case of housing developments.

- General maintenance, including grass cutting.

When a development is completed, a maintenance company is employed by the developer to take care of the services. Each owner of a residential unit becomes a member of the company. Represented as a management committee the residents hold meetings on a regular basis and make decisions as to the better management of the particular development as well as increasing the service charge levied on each house or apartment owner when required in order to cover increased costs for such outlay as insurance or private garbage collection.

All buyers of property in such developments must be under no illusion that when they sign on the dotted line to purchase their new home, they are buying into an annual cost which, some residents complain, continues to spiral. In terms of living in an apartment block, it may rank as a small cost for the security that it brings. In the case of a new housing development, it seems to be an unnecessary cost for the provision of a limited service that, many would argue, should be provided by the local authority. Hard-pressed first-time buyers and others would be relieved of having to face an additional expense, especially during the first few years when money is very tight.

ONE-OFF HOUSES

The thousands of one-off houses scattered throughout the countryside bear witness to the efforts of many people to build their own home to their own design in their chosen location. This, obviously, is not an option for every potential home-owner, even though there is the added benefit that they could save many thousands of Euros by taking this route. Many people who build their own home do so on land acquired from their family. Because of the planning permission restrictions pertaining to the building of one-off houses in some counties, it is advisable to look for outline planning permission for a particular site as a preliminary step and especially before a site is purchased or transferred. These planning restrictions are very controversial in some counties on the eastern and western seaboard in particular and are dealt with elsewhere in this book.

As well as getting planning permission from the local planning authority, it will also be necessary at a very early stage to contact lending institutions to see how much money can be borrowed. What we advised about finding a potential lender in the general situation also applies in this case also. Once it becomes clear how much can be borrowed, an architect can be approached to draw up plans. In this regard, individuals must 'cut their cloth according to their measure,' and the amount of money they qualify for will determine the size and design of the house. Lenders, who would probably provide 90% of the cost of the finished house, including the cost of the site, will require certain documentation. This will include:

- The house plans and specifications.
- Site map.

- Letter showing planning permission
- Letter from borrower's architect or engineer stating they will supervise the development.
- Detailed construction costs.

The lender will detail a surveyor to inspect the site, review the plans and appraise the house for the purposes of *their* investment. The building will be financed through stage payments under which the lender will release the money in stages during construction. This is something which the Law Society does not favour because of the risk associated with the builder becoming insolvent after receiving part of the money and before the house is completed. However, as different stages are completed and certified by the architect (or engineer) supervising the development, the lender will release part of the money.

Borrowers should ensure that they are only paying interest on the amount borrowed at any one time during construction, not on the total amount of the loan. The final amount will be paid out when the lender's surveyor completes a final inspection. The architect, who supervised the building, will complete a certificate of compliance with the planning permission granted for the property.

Again, as with other private house or apartment purchases, the solicitor acting for the borrower will do all things necessary to ensure that the client is fully protected by among other things as getting good title to the land on which the house is built, ensuring that the builder is covered under, what the Law Society considers to be, a limited HomeBond Scheme, and complies with the contract in all material respects. The Law Society has issued many practice notes to its members, warning of the shortcomings of stage payments. Therefore, it is absolutely essential that a solicitor is engaged as early as possible to ensure that the borrower is fully protected from the outset.

Chapter 3

FUNDING THE PURCHASE

'Mortgages, like people, come in different shapes and sizes.' So said the advertising blurb of a major building society this year. It is true, they do and that is why a buyer needs good advice in choosing the one that is suited to a person's individual requirements. Whatever type is suitable, it might be wise move to get **approval before** a deposit is paid on a property, the reason being that it will give the prospective purchaser a good idea of how much he/she can afford. It is not essential that this be done but it gives the buyer solid information in terms of how much they can spend.

RELIEF FOR SELLER

It affords considerable relief to a **seller** of property to be told that the buyer has received mortgage approval or is already in funds after selling their own house. A seller of property does not want to become involved in a chain, whereby the person buying needs to sell their own property before being able to complete the purchase. Still, such chains are part and parcel of the market. However, the last thing a buyer wants is to go on expensive **bridging finance** because of a delay in selling their own property, as can happen all too often in the case of older properties or a sluggish market.

On the other hand, even if loan approval is **not** obtained initially, and the buyer goes ahead and pays a deposit on a house or apartment and it later transpires they cannot afford, the deposit can be returned before contracts are exchanged. It is usually at this latter stage that buyers will seek loan approval.

CHANGED MARKET

The day when a lending institution will charge a mortgage applicant a fee of about €200 just to make an application is, hopefully, long gone. There is too much competition among lenders for any one of them to demand such a charge from an applicant for a mortgage. Therefore, a potential borrower may apply to several lending institutions for approval. Hopefully, when the approvals come back in a couple of days, at the longest, the buyer will have various **terms** and **rates** in writing. These can then be compared in comfort in order to secure the best deal possible.

Although the buyer will now be armed with the fixed and variable interest rates of a number of financial institutions, these rates do not represent the **real** rate. The real rate is called the **Annual Percentage Rate** (APR) and there was a time when this rate was only known to the lender. Not any more. They are legally obliged to give it under the Consumer Credit Act 1995. But what is it? It is the cost of credit on a yearly basis, expressed as a percentage. It includes the up-front charges, if any, paid to obtain the loan. It will take account of all commitments and is usually a higher amount than the interest rate stipulated in the mortgage approval letter. If the APR is not notified by a lender, a buyer should ask for it. Otherwise, the true cost of the borrowing will remain unknown to the buyer.

Potential buyers should make a habit of checking out the property supplements in the newspapers for the various rates. This is an invaluable and easy-to-follow guide to finding the best offers available every week. Perhaps a **tracker mortgage** is more beneficial than a fixed rate mortgage. Maybe, an ordinary **variable rate mortgage** is a better choice in the long run. Still, there is the **special rate** being offered to first-time buyers, which is worth considering. The rates available at any given time must be studied to find the one most suitable in any given case. The figures as appearing in the newspapers towards the end of any given week, are supplied by the lending agencies. They include the **Permanent TSB, AIB Group, Bank of Ireland Mortgages, Bank of Scotland, EBS Building Society, First Active, ICS Building Society, IIB Homeloans, Irish Nationwide Building Society, National Irish Band** and **Ulster Bank**.

DEFINITION OF FIRST-TIME BUYER

It may be important to know who qualifies as a first-time buyer. It is a person who has not previously bought or, for that matter, built a house in this country and in which the purchaser lived as their main residence. Rent should not have been derived from the residential unit for five years after the date of which it was bought. Some of the benefits that accrue to first-time buyers will be addressed later.

MEETING WITH A FINANCIAL INSTITUTION

At your initial meetings with your bank or building society, the information you are seeking includes the following:

- How much money do you qualify to borrow? This can vary from one financial institution to another, but is usually up to 92% of the value of the residential unit. (In certain limited circumstances, they may advance up to 95% of the cost of the property). The actual amount a person qualifies to get can be calculated on the basis of the homebuyer's income, including overtime, bonuses and commission. It can also be calculated by a multiple of the buyer's income or on the person's net income position. If the buyer and his or her partner are buying together, both of their incomes will be combined, again using a multiple of the larger income with the addition of the smaller income to calculate the amount they qualify to borrow. It all depends on the policy of the particular institution. If the buyer is **self-employed**, the lender will look for the buyer's audited accounts for the previous two or three years. This will give a good indication of the buyer's income and outgoings and their ability to repay the mortgage. The buyer's account-ant usually provides this information to the lender.

- In response to a query for the purposes of this book as to the criteria it directs financial institutions to adopt in granting mortgages, **IFSRA** stated that the **Financial Regulator** had two key concerns in relation to financial institutions, 1. **The protection of the consumer** and 2, **The soundness of the financial institution.**

  - 'From the point of view of financial institutions, we do not set the credentials for mortgage approval, i.e. income multiples, loan-to-value ratios, etc. Our main concern is that institutions should only advance loans that are fully suited to their customers' circumstances and must satisfy themselves that the borrower is in a position to repay.'

- "The 3.5 times salary method was traditionally a practice set by the banks. It was not a guideline issued by the Financial Regulator (and was never issued by the Central Bank when it regulated this area). Banks now use much more sophisticated formulae for calculating how much they will give you for a mortgage. In general, a financial institution's decision regarding how much to lend a customer is not based on a single strict rule, but will be based on ability to pay, credit history, other debts," IFSRA stated.

- Over what period of years is the mortgage required - the longer the period, the lower the repayments. The higher the repayments, the sooner the mortgage will be paid off. A repayment period of 35 years is common in today's market.

- What do they advise in terms of paying back the mortgage – monthly repayments, on the same date each month, based on a fixed interest rate or variable interest rate or a combination of both?

- What will the **repayments** be on the amount borrowed?

- A **booking deposit** will always be paid in respect of new properties. It forms part of the 10% that is usually paid to the seller's solicitor some four to six weeks after the initial payment to the seller's estate agent of a sum as low as €1,000 but which could be, and usually is, several thousands more. A deposit must always be paid when the contracts are formally signed, thereby legally binding both parties. Rather than being paid as a percentage of the purchase prices, the deposit could be expressed as a fixed amount, say €10,000. The decision as to which form it will take is entirely one for the developer and his advisers who, through an estate agent, may be amenable to the buyer paying the deposit in 'easy' stages. In the case of second-hand properties, the normal deposit is 10% of the purchase price. That is the situation, whether it is bought by private treaty or at auction. The booking deposit, which will normally be financed by personal borrowings, forms part of the contract. A receipt for this money will state that the sale is 'subject to contract,' 'subject to title' or similar formula as advised by the solicitor in order to comply with the such requirements as those contained in the Statute of Fraud which stipulates that every contract for the sale of land must be evidenced in writing. In addition, the **three Ps** have to be established i.e. the price, the parties and the property must all be certain. A High Court case on this very issue was concerned with the sale of land in a bar of a Co. Galway hotel following the Galway Races when the writing setting out the three Ps was contained on a cigarette box. The seller, who claimed to be the worse for wear with drink, claimed that no contract existed and that he was unaware of what was taking place the night before but the court upheld the validity of the sale. The Statute of Frauds had been satisfied by the evidence written on the box.

- What are the **other likely costs** that will be incurred, such the **solicitor's fees** of probably €1,000 or more, Crucially the outlay also includes the cost of taking out **life assurance** on the buyer's life. This is primarily to protect the lender's investment in the buyer's property. Should the buyer die prior to the mortgage being repaid in full, the insurance will kick in and indemnify the lender for the outstanding amount of the mortgage. It has to be stated that lenders are slow to inform buyers about this additional cost of insurance. **Buyers should be told what their full outlay will be from the outset.** Sometimes, the buyer will not be told that they must get it until near to the closing, at which stage there are two possible scenarios:

  (1) It can lead to a **delay** in the actual closing for a variety of reasons but principally because the insurer may require the buyer to undergo a full medical examination before assuming the risk. If problems are identified, further delay will ensue.

  (2) In order to save time and to ensure that the closing goes ahead on schedule, it may result in the buyer **having to buy the insurance from the insurer** to which the lender is tied, purely for convenience purposes, of course at possibly a higher cost. Life assurance is relatively inexpensive, especially at possibly a higher cost in the case of non-smokers. In fact, it is probably cheaper today than it was 10 years ago.

- There is another policy of insurance that the lender will insist on - **building insurance** (not contents) on the property being purchased. As prices can vary enormously from insurer to insurer, buyers must not rely on just one quotation but must shop around yet again. It is surprising how much money can be saved by doing so.

- Should the buyer get another policy of insurance which is designed to pay the buyer's mortgage for a maximum of 12 months in each eligible claim? This could prove a welcome lifeline, should certain events happen in the life of the buyer, events such as accident or sickness, involuntary unemployment or one of the seven specified critical illnesses, coronary artery bypass surgery, cancer, heart attack, major organ transplant, stroke, kidney failure and loss of sight or limb. The premium can be added to the mortgage repayment. The benefit of having this policy has proved priceless for buyers with the foresight to have it when disaster struck.

All of these policies, while necessary in themselves, add to the outlay the buyer is faced with meeting every month during the life of the mortgage. On top of that, there are other outlays at this early stage. The lender will require the property to be valued by one of the surveyors on their panel, to see if it is good value for the amount of the mortgage they are advancing. Although the surveyor's report is obtained for the benefit of the lender, the cost of about €130 is levied on the buyer, who cannot rely on this report should a problem arise. The buyer should commission a **structural survey** when purchasing a **second hand property** to make sure that it is structurally sound before any money changes hands. Buying a property that will become a home is an expensive business, and can 'stretch' financially and emotionally a person with the strongest character. It is not going to get any cheaper in the immediate future. A report published in January 2005 stated that the demand for residential property is unlikely to decline significantly over the next two years and that interest rates were forecast to rise by up to three-quarters of a percentage point by the end of 2005.

MISLEADING ADVERTISING
A draft code was issued recently by IFSRA, which aims to protect consumers from misleading advertising. Essentially, it bans financial institutions from offering unsolicited pre-

approved loans. All regulated lenders, including those who provide mortgages, will have to explain in writing why they are recommending a certain product to customers.

In addition, in an effort to stamp out fraudulent applications for home loans, intermediaries must confirm that they have seen original documents such as bank statements, certificate of earnings and P60s that support an individual's application and ability to repay a loan. Buyers also have a responsibility to be truthful in respect of their mortgage applications. The code, expected to be implemented by the end of 2005, provides for the imposition of fines of up to €5 million against lenders found to be in breach of the regulations.

Chapter 4

BUYERS, SELLERS AND VIEWERS BEWARE

As advised earlier 'You buy with a view to selling,' meaning that the time property is purchased is the time that the buyer must be conscious of the fact that it should be marketable and sufficiently well constructed, appointed, located and presented that it can be sold on by that buyer, later. To use a term that had its origins in rural Ireland in the dim and distant past: "**Don't buy a pig in a poke**." However, the most important aspect of all that the buyer must be able to prove, is ownership of the property. If a house, apartment or site for a proposed residential development, has been bought on the basis of a perceived good title but it subsequently transpires that the seller or vendor did not have proper title at all, then the buyer - and, most likely, his solicitor - has a big problem. The seller may only have had possessory title, which is not what any buyer wants. The buyer and his advisers must make sure there are no 'warts' on the title. Nothing less than absolute title is required. In the first place, therefore, it is essential for **sellers or vendors** to establish that they are selling property with good title. If a problem should arise with the title during the course of conveyancing process, it will affect not only the buyer but may lead to the collapse of the sale.

There is a Latin phrase that immediately springs to mind: *nemo dat quod non habet*. Put simply it means, 'I cannot give what I haven't got.' If the vendor does not have good title to the property he is selling, then he cannot sell what he does not own. While this is a matter for the buyer's solicitor to make sure of, one of the purposes of this book is to alert buyers to as many pitfalls as possible that can be encountered along the way. The question of title will be dealt with later.

DON'T JUDGE THE BOOK BY THE COVER

People buying property today need to be up early in the morning –as the saying goes – and be alive to problems that may present themselves as the buying process continues. Things may not always be what they seem. **Caveat emptor** - *Let the buyer beware*. This phrase is well known in the commercial world. Because the purchase of a home is the largest investment most of us make during our lifetime, the warning contained in those two words must have greater significance for us.

A case in point occurred in an East of Ireland town some years ago when a potential buyer decided to move to another location, and came across what he thought was a new house under construction just off the main thoroughfare of a small town. It seemed just what he wanted. The price was right and it was new. In addition, and most important, he would qualify for the first-time buyer's grant then available. The process of purchasing the house was going ahead without any problems until his solicitor discovered, in response to the requisitions or questions he raised with the vendor's solicitor, that he was not buying a 'new' house at all. The reality was that the builder had sold the house earlier during the construction stage to the person now selling the house. It was the vendor who benefited from the grant and was, in fact, selling a second-hand house. As a result, stamp duty was payable on the property. Naturally, the young man who was hoping to make a new life in a country town, was shattered and withdrew immediately from the transaction. It was a salutary lesson that others may learn from - **never to judge the book by the cover**.

LET THE SELLER BEWARE

A problem that crops up from time to time and one that can have devastating effect on people selling their home or apartment is the **theft** of items from the property by viewers. The fact that a person leaves out items of special value such as ornaments and, perhaps, even jewellery, to enhance the appearance of various rooms, can be misguided. It is putting a trust in faceless, and maybe nameless, people who will never 'darken the door' again. It is also imposing a very high degree of vigilance on estate agents and their representatives who could not possibly 'police' every viewer on an occasion when many people may be viewing at the same time, albeit, they could do so when a single viewer is being shown around the property. However, there is an inherent risk in either situation in the event of the agent wrongly challenging somebody's honesty and being subsequently sued for slander.

Learning from the mistakes of other people should be a good lesson for all sellers, not to leave out small items of special value. In addition, estate agents should be more alive to the likelihood of such thefts and exercise greater vigilance of their client's property. When they are in sole charge of a seller's property during a viewing period, they are in the legal position of being a trustee of the property with a consequent legal obligation to their client to ensure its safety. Any breach of that obligation by carelessness, lack of vigilance or otherwise, could leave them open to a successful action by the owner/seller.

MISLEADING ADVERTISING

Advertising blurbs and editorial write-ups in brochures, newspapers and on the Internet are excellent forums for developers and other sellers to get their message of what they are selling out to the public. Advertorials accompanying hard commercial advertising are 'soft' by nature, illustrating only the positive aspects of the property for sale. Some can be downright misleading. Two examples:

A few years ago a family interested in moving out of Dublin were suitably impressed by the lavish write-up accorded to a particular property set on its own land, herb garden, outhouses which could double up as extra bedrooms when visitors arrived, to undertake almost a three-hour journey only to find the shambles of a building masquerading as a house and barns. There was so little relationship between what was portrayed in the national daily newspaper editorial content and what the family found that it justified a complaint being filed with the Advertising Standards Authority (ASA) for misleading advertising, albeit the editorial copy was not contained in an actual advertisement as such. The family concluded that it was a costly waste of an entire day and returned home chastened by the experience, ,and drawing down ire on the newspaper that carried such a misleading write-up. The lesson they learned is one for everybody interested in buying a house: don't be swayed by editorial descriptions of property; check out the facts personally and make up your own mind after taking expert advice.

- An estate agent selling news houses on the southern cross road on the outskirts of Bray, Co. Wicklow used a large colourful brochure with a picture of a seaside harbour, complete with moored boats, as a selling point. The only thing wrong with this was that the harbour was not in Bray, as potential buyers would expect being a seaside town but in the next town south, Greystones, about four miles away – surely a case of misleading buyers into thinking that they were buying a house with such a picturesque a harbour on their very doorstep. Again, there is no substitute for an on-site visit to establish the exact location.

- Housing and apartment developments all tend to be described as 'luxurious' in the advertising copy paid for by the developer with superb locations, within walking distance of schools, shops, public transport. What more could a potential buyer want? **Buyer beware**!

INSPECTIONS

Buying a house or apartment is not a time for half measures. In order to try and fully insure against unpleasant surprises

-when it may be too late to withdraw from the purchase-there should be an inspection of the **property** by either a chartered surveyor, an architect or an engineer. In the case of a property already constructed, the survey should be carried out *before* contracts are exchanged. However, if the apartment or house is under construction, the best advice is to have it inspected while the building work is in progress and most definitely again just before completion. Even if the inspection during the actual building work is not done, it is imperative that one be carried out before the sale is closed. If the property is a site, a similar inspection should be carried out to establish that the site is suitable for the development in terms of drainage, land levels and services, such as water supply and sewage, especially if the buyer is faced with drilling on the site for water and installing a septic tank.

The '**Site for sale**' sign that may have attracted the buyer in the first place may not have disclosed that the site was 'land-locked', and could only be reached by means of a right-of-way through a neighbour's property… a disastrous situation and one that must be avoided at all costs. The buyer's professional advisers will establish whether the property has access to the public road or is land-locked, or whether it is, itself, the subject of an easement such as a right-of-way. Crucially, if it is a house in a rural location, the source of its water supply needs to be established. It may be supplied from a well located on the land of a neighbour who had never charged for this service, but had recently died, and the new owner had served notice of intent to charge for it.

A similar situation occurred in a rural setting in the West of Ireland a few years ago when, following the demise of the owner of land with a well which had supplied a local group water supply for years, the new owner served notice of intent to charge each householder about €5,000 a year for the water. Attempts at negotiating a lower charge for the water failed, and the householders in the scheme made plans to arrange to get connected to a new supply of their own. They estimated their total outlay would be in the region of a one off payment of about €5,000 per house or less. Building a house in the countryside might sound idyllic, but the project needs to be researched minutely from every possible angle before a single Euro is spent.

THE PLANNING LAND MINE

Planning strategies and policies adopted by some county councils throughout the country are a controversial subject, in that they are seen by many to interfere too much in the plans of people to build in the countryside. Take the case of a person who wishes to move from an urban to a rural setting and to build their own house on a site in Co. Wicklow, probably the most contentious of all counties in this respect, or in one of the counties along the Western seaboard, like **Galway** (particularly in **Connemara**) or **Clare**. The policies favour the **natives** above all others, a fact that must be proved to the planning authorities.

To give an idea of how restrictive it can be for an '**outsider**', the following extract from the **Co. Wicklow Development Plan** for 2004-2010, which states, in part, that residential development will be **considered** only when it is for the provision of "**a necessary dwelling**" in the following circumstances:

- A **permanent native resident** seeking to build for his/her own family and not as speculation. A permanent native resident shall be a person who was either born and reared in the family home in the immediate vicinity of the proposed site, or resided in the immediate environs of the proposed site for **at least 10 consecutive years prior to the application for planning permission**.

- **A son or daughter, or niece/nephew** considered to merit the same position as son/daughter within the law (i.e. when the uncle/aunt has no children of his/her own), of a permanent native resident of a rural area, who can **demonstrate a definable social or economic need to live in the area** in which the proposal relates and not as speculation.

- A son or daughter, or niece/nephew considered to merit the same position as a son/daughter within the law (i.e. when the uncle/aunt has no children of his/her own), of a permanent native resident of a rural area, **whose place of employment is outside the immediate environs of the local rural area** in which the application relates, and who can demonstrate a definable social or economic need to live in the area to which the proposal relates and not as speculation.

- Replacing a farm dwelling for the **needs of a farming family,** not as speculation.

- A person whose **principle occupation is in agriculture**, and who owns and farms substantial lands in the immediate vicinity of the site.

- An **immediate family member** (i.e. son or daughter) of a person just described, who is occupied in agriculture in the immediate vicinity.

- A person whose principle occupation is in a **rural resource-based activity** (i.e. agriculture, forestry, mariculture, agri-tourism etc.), and who can demonstrate a need to live in the immediate vicinity of this activity.

- **Renovation or conversion of existing dilapidated buildings of substance** in a scale, density and manner appropriate to the rural area and its scenic amenities. Any such developments shall be in accordance with the **Wicklow Rural Residential Guidelines** (these are set out in a different section of the Development Plan).

- **A close relative who has inherited,** either as a gift or on death, an agricultural holding or site for his/her own purposes and not for speculation and who can demonstrate a definable social and or economic need to live in the area to which the proposal relates.

- A permanent native resident who has to **dispose** of their dwelling on foot of a court order following a divorce or a legal separation.

- **The son or daughter of a landowner who has inherited a site** for the purpose of building a one-off rural house and where the land has been in family ownership as at October 11, 2004 for at least 10 years prior to the application for planning permission and not as speculation.

- An **emigrant**, returning to their local area, seeking to build a house for his/her own use and not as speculation.

- Persons whose **work is intrinsically linked to the rural area** and who can prove a definable social and economic need to live in the rural area and who has resided in the immediate area for at least 10 consecutive years prior to the application

- Permanent native residents of primary and secondary growth centres, seeking to build a house in their native town or village within the 30 mph (50 km/h) speed limit on the non-national radial roads, for their own use and not as speculation, as of October 11, 2004.
  (*All of the emphasis in bold in the above planning section are those of the author*).

However, the restrictions do not end there. Other limits are applied. Where permission is granted for the development of a dwelling in the countryside of Wicklow, the planning authority will seek the applicant's agreement to enter into an agreement under **section 47 of the Local Government (Planning and Development) Act 2000,** restricting occupation of the dwelling to the applicant, his or her heirs, or those persons described above and others listed, or other classes of persons as the planning authority might agree to.

There are also restrictions on the type of **house design,** which must adhere to the principles and objectives of the **Wicklow Rural Residential Guidelines** and the criteria for **Residential Development in Landscape Zones**. Permissions for developments within "high vulnerability landscape areas of outstanding natural beauty" are subject to a visual impact assessment. Wicklow Planning Authority receives more than 100 planning applications each month, and an estimated 60% of these would be for one-off houses in the countryside.

Is it any wonder that a person who satisfies the planners and obtains permission to build a one-off house of their choice and design in the countryside of Co. Wicklow must feel as if they had won the **Lotto**! However, there is nothing to stop a person buying one of the many new homes in small housing developments that are frequently coming on the market, not only in Co. Wicklow, but also throughout rural Ireland.

Chapter 5

PRIVATE TREATY V. PUBLIC AUCTION

PRIVATE TREATY

When a potential buyer does find a suitable property to call home, contact will have to be made with the estate agent who is looking after the sale and place an offer on it, that is if the seller employed the services of one at all. Increasingly, people with residential units to sell are putting advertisements on the Internet and trying their luck with selling the property themselves.

This is particularly the case with houses valued up to €400,000. An average of anything between 0.75% and 1.5% of the cost price can be saved by **sellers** using this method of selling, because the fee the seller can expect to pay the estate agent handling the sale would be within that range. If they have the time and confidence required to meet prospective buyers and show them around their property, there no reason why they can't achieve a sale with very low advertising costs to worry about.

The popularity of this type of sale is not only confined to this country, but it has caught on to such an extent in England that estate agents are expressing concerns at the loss of potential business. There not only does a seller get to advertise their property on the website for a small fee but the people who operate the sites come out, where required, and put up a board to advertise the property.

In Ireland, the website www.daft.ie is very popular. An acquaintance placed a small notice on this website earlier this year for a house being offered for sale in Co. Dublin. Within 24 hours, two calls expressing an interest were received. A day later, one of the interested parties went round, viewed the property, asked plenty of questions of the seller and then paid a deposit of €5,000 on a purchase price of just under €400,000 for the house. A nice, clean and cheap private treaty sale. All at the unbelievable cost of €85. A solicitor was engaged immediately to look after the seller's interest and see the sale to a conclusion. In the event of the sale falling through with the first potential buyer, there were a number of others on stand-by. There is a lesson in there for sellers, to make sure that a list of people who inquired about the property is retained as a contingency.

ESTATE AGENTS

"If you can't beat them, join them," appears to be the motto of hundreds of estate agents. They also advertise their clients' property on this and similar website. Why not! It is another forum that potential buyers have been checking since it was set up about eight years ago. Estate agents will never lose their popularity for handling the sale of houses, apartment and land. They are still the preferred option for most sellers and buyers. They are using the website to good effect, no doubt. Yet another forum for buyers to browse is the website of the estate agents themselves, www.myhome.ie, which is heavily used. Buyers now automatically log on to this website in the hunt for potential properties. Apart from advertising properties on this website, many individual estate agents also have their own website which they use to good effect. Another website is www.realestate.ie and yet another is www.nicemove.ie. Searching websites has become, and will continue to be, a fruitful exercise for many buyers. Apart from the regular newspapers, yet another useful tool that potential buyers should check for a house or apartment is *Buy and Sell*. Sellers will use every possible medium to find a buyer and one who will pay the most money. Therefore, every avenue must be explored by buyers in their quest.

Despite the apparent financial saving to the vendor by using the internet to sell the property, an estate agent would argue that higher prices will be achieved for property by a vendor engaging their services rather than relying on one's own negotiating skills which, after all, are amateurish in contrast to those of a professional. In addition, they are in a position to make judgments on the **genuineness** of potential buyers and their ability to come up with the **finance** sooner rather than later. In addition, they have the negotiation skills to "talk" the potential buyer into possibly paying more for the property than might otherwise be the case. These are just some of the reasons why the vast majority of sales are handled by estate agents.

BEWARE THE "DUTCH AUCTION"

Equipped with the knowledge and, possibly, a **Letter of Offer** stating that a chosen lender will advance three, four or even five times a person's income by way of a mortgage, the potential buyer, will make an offer of €x for a property to an the estate agent handling the sale for the vendor. He or she may have to wait hours or maybe a day or two for a response as to whether the offer is acceptable to the vendor who, it must be remembered, is taking advice at all time from the estate agent. While ostensibly the agent you contact with your offer appears sympathetic to the offer, the agent will be making a considered judgment as to whether he or she thinks the buyer is prepared to bid a higher sum of money for the property. The **seller** will be advised accordingly by the agent. Buyers must never lose sight of the fact that the more the agent achieves for the vendor, the more he will get in commission, unless a specific sum of money rather than commission on the sale was agreed between the seller and the agent at the outset. The estate agent, therefore, has a **vested interest** in getting as high a price as possible for the seller.

When the seller is happy that the best price has been offered and is unlikely to be topped, the agent is officially informed that the offer is being accepted. The agent will then communicate the good news to the buyer. That is normally the end of the invitation to treat stage or negotiations. However, it often happens that there are a number of people interested in buying the property. It just takes two interested parties to push up the price. One will make a fresh offer to the seller's agent and this is communicated to the other interested party who may put a higher bid to the agent. The other party is informed of this by the agent who then receives a higher bid from that party. And on it goes, with the price going higher and higher, depending on how much each of the parties can afford to offer or, maybe, cannot afford. Perhaps, it is a case of the 'heart ruling the head,' of common sense being put to one side by a decision not to be outdone by an unseen bidder. It is natural for the parties at some stage in that bidding process, which is known as a '**Dutch auction**,' to wonder if they were being '**led up the garden path**' by an estate agent. Was there another bidder at all?

TRUE STORY

Fact is stranger than fiction. The author and his wife found themselves in this very position more than 20 years ago, and can testify to having had those very feelings when informed by the agent for the vendor that their offer had been bettered by another party interested in buying the same Georgian house built on the Southside of Dublin city in the 1830s. An increased offer to the agent was again topped by the other side. Did they exist or was it a put-up by the agent? We had no way of knowing. On and on it went until, in fairness, the agent called a halt to the bidding and came up with a solution that satisfied both parties – we should attend a city centre hotel and bid against each other for the house.

PRIVATE AUCTION

On the appointed day, in the formality of a public auction, the **conditions of the sale** were read out by the auctioneer to the author, who was accompanied by his solicitor **and** the other bidder, a man and his wife. So, they really did exist. It was genuine. The auctioneer said he would take bids and the author's solicitor then made an opening bid at the price at which the property was advertised by the estate agent. We waited with baited breath for the other party to make their counterbid but, in fact, there was an unbelievable silence. They didn't make a bid. Instead, they announced that they were withdrawing and crossed the room and shook hands with us. Why had they gone to the trouble of attending the auction if they were not going to bid? The reason they gave was that they shared the same suspicion as we did, that the estate agent was merely 'puffing' up the price for his own and his client's ends and that we did not exist as a competing bidder at all. Nothing could have been further from the truth. They acted entirely honourably throughout but, human nature being what it is, we both felt the other did not exist. All doubts were dispelled in an instant. Smiles and handshakes all round, a cheque for 10% of the price at which the house was 'knocked down' at was drawn there and then and it was time for celebration.

Is it always so? Are all estate agents so honourable that they would not 'puff' the price for their own and their client's purposes by creating an artificial 'Dutch auction'? Without actually knowing the correct answer to that question, suffice to say that thinking as a lawyer and basing an answer to it on the civil standard of proof 'on the balance of probabilities,' I would say they are not; that there are people who suffered financially and emotionally and paid over the odds for the home they were after because such a practice was used by an estate agent. It is not illegal. Equally, it would not have been illegal or unlawful in any way for the agent involved in the situation outlined above to have had a third party planted in the hotel room to make a counter bid, if necessary, in order to achieve a higher bid from the genuine bidders. Is such a practice ethical? The vendor would respond that it was but the bidder would say it was not, cry 'foul,' and say it smacked of sharp practice and should be condemned.

BUYING BY TENDER – 'BEST AND FINAL OFFER'
As stated above, people are suspicious by nature, especially when there is money at stake and it appears that the playing

pitch is uneven for all the players. Take for instance the situation that arises when a number of potential buyers for a house or apartment, who have been bidding against each other in communication with the seller's agent, are asked to submit their final offer in a sealed envelope. They are told individually that the highest bid will secure the property. The deadline for receipt of these tenders arrives and the estate agent duly opens the envelopes out of sight of all the potential buyers and ascertains the one containing the highest bid. Once satisfied that all appears to be in order, the agent will notify the successful highest bidder and that is that.

However, what happens if the agent is less than scrupulously fair and decides privately that the second highest bidder will get the house or apartment. Perhaps the second highest bidder may have come to some private arrangement with the agent. Who is to know the truth? The truth, in fact, may never be known and the person who should have secured the property will be left 'in the dark.' Without in any way impugning the honest of estate agents, is there not a case to be made that in all such bidding by tender situations that the **bidders should have a representative present as witness** to the opening of the envelopes and the declaration of the winner on merit? The question posed here should be answered in the affirmative to ensure **full transparency**, for both sellers and buyers.

PUBLIC AUCTION

There are **benefits** to selling and buying by public auction. Assuming that a property comes on the market for sale by public auction, different considerations apply - some of benefit, some not so. On the plus side, the person interested in buying will have up to three or even four weeks in which to minutely go through the property, have it completely surveyed, obtain loan approval up to a limit and have answers obtained from the seller's advisers with regard to the property. It gives an opportunity to check out the neighbourhood and the facilities, including shops, schools if necessary, and public transport, Equally, for the seller's solicitor, there is ample time to have the necessary documents prepared and the **contract** drawn up for execution on the day of the auction. The seller will have opted for public auction on the advice of the estate agent on the basis, perhaps, that it was a unique building because of its type, location or both and would therefore be expected to fetch a high price. Equally, the estate agent will have gauged the market and will know if there will be lively interest in the property at a public auction.

While a person buying by private treaty may have conditions imposed by the seller, such as not being allowed to buy as part of a chain (i.e. the buyer having to first sell their own property before closing the purchase), or having to complete the purchase by a certain date, the person who successfully bids for a property at a public auction will also have to abide by certain conditions of sale. Prepared by the seller's solicitor, these will be read out by the auctioneer or, in some cases, by the seller's solicitor, when the auction gets under way and are not subject to negotiation after the property is knocked down to the highest bidder. The format for the conditions of sale used at an auction is the very same as that used in a private treaty sale. The only difference will be the general conditions as applied to the auction itself.

The Law Society has drawn up a printed form of contract, which is always used. The successful bidder cannot impose any conditions such as making the purchase subject to loan approval, or being tied to the sale of their own property before completion, or of a satisfactory survey of the property being obtained. The buyer's solicitor will also be informed by the seller's solicitor if there are any notices affecting the property such as, for example, a Compulsory Purchase Order (CPO) or road construction by the local authority. If the seller and his or her advisers try to mislead a buyer by camouflaging the reality of a CPO and the sale goes through, then the buyer may be left with no option but to bring a claim in the High Court to have the sale **rescinded** on the basis of an alleged misrepresentation.

The buyer's solicitor will also establish if there are debts registered against the property. If there are, they must be discharged by the seller from the proceeds of sale and not by the buyer. It is **extremely important** that a bidder at a public auction should be accompanied by their solicitor, who is well accustomed to attending and bidding at auctions on behalf of clients. When it is necessary, they will buy in trust for a client whose identity will not be revealed.

This is not the time for half-measures by the prospective buyer. His or her solicitor will ensure that no unnecessary burdens, in the form of conditions, are being imposed by the seller, will protect his or her client during the actual bidding process and subsequently, in an adjoining room when the contract is signed and the cheque for the deposit is handed over to the seller's solicitor. There are many other issues that the buyer's solicitor will work on to protect his client's interests and, most important of all, to make sure that the buyer is getting good title.

COMPARATIVE COSTS

People with properties in the higher price category are usually best advised to sell by public auction rather than by private treaty. The **cost of advertising jumps** considerably as block advertising is usually used as well as the cost of erecting signs at the property and preparing and printing brochures. An estimated €3,000 is set aside for advertising, that is about €700 and VAT for an advertisement with photograph in a daily or Sunday newspaper, to appear on three successive weeks. The estate agent may also succeed in getting some editorial copy about the property into the newspapers in which he or she advertises the property. However, some newspapers might insist on exclusivity in terms of getting all the advertising for a property before agreeing to provide editorial space for 'a write-up.' The estate agent provides the necessary information about the property and the newspaper arranges for a staff or freelance journalist to write the copy to a format known as the house style. The editorial is provided free of charge as such. The estate agent will have employed a professional photographer to photograph the property for a fee of about €300 plus VAT. It is this carefully crafted advertising and editorial material describing the most **positive aspects** of the house or apartment, coupled with colourful pictures that will attract the interest of buyers.

Whereas the estate agent's fees will be agreed at from 0.75% upwards of the price achieved in a private treaty sale, it is likely that fees of 1.5% of the price reached at auction will be charged to the vender selling by public auction. For a landmark property, the fee might be higher or, indeed, much lower as estate agents secure valuable publicity to enhance their reputation in the market place for handling such properties.

Should the property fail to reach the level known as the **reserve** or the value put on the property by the seller, it may then be **withdrawn** or else, and more likely, be put on the market as a private treaty sale. If this is what transpires, the attendant costs, made up of the considerable advertising costs, will become payable by the seller. Should this happen, it is very much to the benefit of the highest bidder at the auction, who may be invited by the auctioneer to make a fresh offer in private. The property can often be bought at a much lower price than that being sought at the public auction. However, **if the buyer succeeds** in getting the property during the bidding process in today's competitive market with lots of money apparently available for expensive houses, it may be at a high price. Competition from other bidders dictates what the eventual price will be. Market forces dictate that there are few bargains to be got at public auctions.

Chapter 6

WHEN THE OFFER IS ACCEPTED

SECOND-HAND PROPERTIES

Some items, such as curtains, carpets, light fittings or furniture, which were in the house or apartment during the viewing, could be included in the contract under a heading known as '**special conditions**' in the conditions of sale. These may or may not have been specifically included following negotiation between the seller and the buyer during the negotiations. There could be other special conditions in a contract for sale, which were inserted by the vendor's solicitor, for example, requiring a closing of the sale within a specified time. All of this should act as a pointer to potential buyers that if they want some of the fittings included as part of the sale price, they should seek the agreement of the vendor to this. (See also Chapter 12.)

Including one or more items in the sale price can be a good **bargaining tool for a seller** The vendor may have been experiencing sluggish interest in the property and may be hard-pressed to find a buyer. If a potential buyer comes along, shows a willingness to buy but expresses a special interest in having certain items included, it would be a foolish vendor who would refuse such a request. In other words, the items would be included in the sale at no extra cost The last thing a vendor should do is to get 'hung-up' and lose a willing buyer for the sake of some second-hand goods. After all, that is all they are, used property, which may have seen better days but which would be more than welcome by a buyer who will be 'counting the pennies' for many a day, unable to afford to buy new carpets, new curtains or maybe a cooker or dishwasher. Once the buyer is **reasonable** as to what is requested, there should be no difficulty in reaching agreement as part of the purchase price itself.

There is a variation on this situation, which is of greater benefit to the vendor than to the buyer. This relates to a situation where the fittings the buyer wants becomes the subject of a collateral or secondary agreement (for a definition of **'fixtures'** and **'fittings'** see **Glossary**). The buyer will pay the vendor for the items, but it will be over and above what is being paid for the property. A buyer can therefore see the benefit of trying to have them included as part of the purchase price itself.

NEW PROPERTIES

The only way to relate this situation to a new property is when a **showhouse** or **show apartment** is being sold fully furnished and the buyer wants to buy the house 'as is.' Developers and their agents are often prepared to do business with such buyers provided they pay for what are usually modern, state-of-the-art furnishings, furniture and kitchen appliances specially selected for the showhouse by special designers. Sometimes, it is possible for a buyer to negotiate the price for these to be included in the overall price for the property. To buy a showhouse is invariably more expensive as fixtures and fittings are included in the sale price, which is usually more than comparable that of a property.

TWO DEPOSITS

Sometimes, a buyer will be surprised when told by his solicitor or by the estate agent selling a new property that he or she has to pay more than one deposit. In fact, there may be two sets of contracts in a situation where new houses are being built in a housing estate. They will be signed together but the respective deposits when combined should not amount to more than 10% of the cost of the purchase price. It is usual for the builder to enter into two agreements, one for the transfer of the site and the other, a building agreement, under which the builder agrees to construct a house on the site transferred. The documents that are used in these transactions are generally standard. The one currently in use was agreed between the **Construction Industry Federation** and the **Law Society** in the mid 1980s. It is one of the most important of all documents involved in the entire transaction, containing as it does the obligations and responsibilities of the builder and the buyer, in building the house and paying for it, respectively. The buyer's solicitor will provide ample advice on the transaction for the buyer as the process progresses.

THE DEPOSIT IS NOW PAID

Deposits are not refundable once the once the contracts are signed. It should be noted that a deposit may be paid directly to the builder if it is a member of the **HomeBond scheme**. This which indemnifies the buyer against the loss of the deposit on a new property or stage payments because the building company goes into liquidation or, in the case of an individual builder, goes bankrupt. If they have not already done so - and they should have - the buyer should immediately **engage a solicitor** to look after the legalities of the purchase, and a financial institution to arrange a mortgage. The many issues which need attention at this stage, include:

- Protecting the buyer's deposit by ensuring that the deposit will be returned, if the buyer withdraws from the purchase. While most people know that a deposit will be refunded, the author and his wife, as first-time buyers, were forced to engage solicitor and counsel many years ago to issue a Circuit Court civil bill to secure the return of their deposit after the builder **failed, refused or neglected** (the wording of the civil bill) to return the deposit. It was immediately returned after the court document was served.

- **Insert a condition** in the contract to free the buyer from the deal if he or she fails to get mortgage approval from a financial institution. While it is not unusual for one or more lenders to turn down an application, for any number of reasons but most likely due to an inadequate regular income, it is extremely important from a legal perspective to protect the prospective buyer from being sued to complete the purchase. Also, the buyer's solicitor will ensure that the vendor has not included a condition that is difficult for the buyer to comply with.

- Exercise legal vigilance over any **special conditions** put in by the vendor such as, in the case of a second-hand property, to accept the property in its present condition. Does that mean there is a problem such as subsidence, a crack in a gable wall, dry rot or some such apparent calamity? While the solicitor will put specific questions regarding such a condition, he will not just rely on the responses he gets from the vendor but will advise his client to engage a surveyor to carry out a thorough **structural survey** of the property. Of course, it is prudent to have such a survey carried out where an older property is concerned.

- Resist the inclusion by the vendor in the building agreement of a price variation clause, unless the buyer agrees with it. If permitted to remain, it would allow the builder to increase the cost of the property to cover an increase in materials or labour or both.

- If the property is second-hand, the condition of the walls, floors, roof, windows, electric wiring and so on must be examined. An architect, engineer or chartered surveyor may discover severe woodworm infestation or rising damp in the ground floor walls, which will require costly specialist treatment. This discovery goes into the surveyor's report and will be acted on by the buyer's advisers, who will inform the vendor accordingly. There are **three possible outcomes** - the buyer may withdraw altogether, scared off by the possible cost of treating the walls for the dampness or of the possibility of the greater damage it will cause if allowed to go unabated; try and get the vendor to carry out the remedial work before the purchase is completed or, thirdly, bargain with the vendor to reduce the purchase price of the property by the full amount of having the remedial work carried out by the buyer after taking possession. A report from an expert giving full costings of the reinstatement would be required by the buyer in order to prove or vouch the cost involved. This last of the three options is probably the most likely outcome, if the vendor **needs** to sell badly enough and the buyer **wants** the particular property.

- If it is a new house that is under construction, the buyer needs to exercise personal vigilance for any change or modification that might be made to the house as purchased. While many builders will not allow unauthorised persons – including the buyer - other than those involved in the construction, including sub-contractors and suppliers, into the house during actual building operations for insurance or other reasons, opportunities should still be looked out for in order to get a closer look. If something untoward appears to be happening, such as an unauthorised variation in the **planning permission** granted to the developer or in the **plans and specifications** for the house, the buyer's solicitor must be advised of this to take up the issue with the developer's solicitor as a matter of urgency. Ideally, the plans and specification should be handed over before the contracts are issued so that monitoring can begin earlier, albeit the plans are usually available for **viewing only** in the showhouse. It might be too late when they are issued with the contracts. Also, it may be too late to right a wrong by the time they are issued with the contracts, or when it is time for the snag list to be drawn up near the end. Of course, it is always possible for changes to be made by agreement between the parties.

- Buyers of new houses and apartments should seek any changes they want to be made as early as possible. These might include something as basic as extra power points. A house or apartment can never have enough of them. It costs about €70 to have one installed and it is probably cheaper and cleaner to have it done during this early stage than later when construction is completed.

- The stages at which the balance of the purchase money should be paid together with the closing date and the timeframe allowed to the buyer to make complaints about defects will be in the agreement and may need to be altered according to the legal and financial advice received by the buyer. The closing date depends on when the new house is completed and could vary from two weeks to 18 months or even longer from the date the contract is signed. Most of the minor repairs, such as remedying sloppy plastering, unfinished painting, tiles not grouted properly, lumps of plaster left on wooden floors, will be picked up when the snag list is being prepared by a surveyor, engineer or architect but other defects may not be spotted until the buyer moves in. This could include cracks appearing in walls, plumbing problems, central heating working only spasmodically. Some of these, especially the cracked walls, have the potential to be serious. While most building agreements allow for a period of six months for complaints about what might be termed 'minor defects' to be made by the buyer, such agreements usually allow up to 10 years for major problems to be brought to the attention of the developer for attention. Possible subsidence, cracks appearing on walls and maybe the chimney, if there is one on the house, the sewerage system constantly blocking, window frames letting in wind and rain and cracks appearing in timber doors, which may indicate that they were not adequately dried of moisture, could be classed as major defects, if serious enough.

- The **HomeBond** scheme, mentioned above, guarantees a house against major structural defects for 10 years. It also guarantees the house for the first two years of its life against smoke and water penetration. The buyer's solicitor will check to ensure that the builder is a member of the **National House Building Guarantee Co. Ltd** through which the guarantee scheme operates.

- In the case of a second-hand house, the closing may vary from four to six weeks from the date the contract is signed. Usually, it is one calendar month. Again, the buyer may be able to get it delayed for a reasonable period of say, one or two weeks, by advancing a good reason.

- Also, in the case of a second-hand house, the vendor's solicitor or estate agent will hold the deposit as **stakeholder** until completion. This can be unnecessarily contentious from the point of view of buyers who claim that the stakeholder is getting the interest on the deposit. There should be no cause for concern in today's climate as the deposit interest rates ensure that the 'return' on the average deposit for such a short period is measured in cents rather than Euro. Stamp duty is payable on second-hand properties and also on house sites in certain circumstances (see chapter 10).

No two purchases work out exactly the same. There is many a slip between cup and lip' and, in normal circumstances, what can be termed 'hiccups' will occur, no matter how much homework the buyer does in saving for the deposit, engaging the specialist services of various advisers, taking and acting on expert advice and being generally vigilant as to what should be done from the start of the viewing and buying process. One can only do their best to prepare but it can be a very stressful experience, particularly as the completion stage draws closer.

Chapter 7

CHOOSING A SOLICITOR

Whether you are buying or selling a property, you will need a solicitor. While you may be able to dispose of, or purchase, your house or apartment without the assistance of an estate agent, it will not be possible to complete successfully the very serious legal procedures involved in such a transaction without engaging a solicitor, not just any solicitor but a solicitor who specialises in conveyancing.

CONVEYANCING

What is conveyancing, which is a word that many may be familiar with, without knowing what it means? According to a definition published by the Law Society of Ireland, it is "the sum of the procedures used in the **disposal and acquisition** of immovable property. It is the procedural side of the coin of which the law of property is the substantive side." It goes on:

> "Conveyancers are the qualified professionals retained by the parties to a transaction to ensure the proper disposal and acquisition of the title to the property involved and to secure the mortgage or charge of any lending institution involved. In Ireland, conveyancing for reward can only be carried out by qualified solicitors."

This monopoly has been challenged as being anti-competitive by the Competition Authority.

Anybody, or almost anybody, can process their own divorce application, including representing themselves before a judge in the Circuit Court. Despite the gravity of preparing for, and asking, a court to dissolve a marriage, it does not require any legal training to put together the documents necessary to make the application, and the financial cost is almost negligible. Anybody, without the necessary legal training, who might consider taking it upon themselves to process a transfer of title in their **own** case would, according to the old saying, **'have a fool for a client'** not least because if a lay person, as such, takes on the task and gets it wrong, they have no redress. In addition, the financial institution providing the mortgage would veto such a move, on this ground alone.

Not every solicitor practices conveyancing, even though every qualified solicitor has to undergo vigorous training in the subject as a student in the Society's Law School. Some solicitors practice exclusively in the area of intellectual property such as copyright, trademarks and designs. Others devote their practice solely to criminal law, while others might engage in a mixed practice of litigation, including family law, criminal law and, perhaps conveyancing. Some devote their entire practice to conveyancing. Individual solicitors within a given practice run by a group of solicitors acting in a legal partnership may each have their own area of speciality, but whatever the type of practice the solicitor is engaged in, whether in an urban and rural setting, the buyer or seller of property must engage one who practices conveyancing.

CHOOSING YOUR SOLICITOR: A CAVEAT
In deciding what solicitor to engage, there is one big **caveat** that must be emphasised: **under no circumstances** must the same solicitor act for both the seller and the buyer in the respect of the same property transaction, no matter how attractive this arrangement might seem from a cost saving perspective for both parties. The reason for this is that a potential **conflict of interest** situation could arise as a result of which the interests of one party could only be served by having the exclusive services of his or her own solicitor. He or she would be exclusively acting in the best interests of the wife, something that the original solicitor, with the best will in the world, could not do because of the fact that he was trying to serve both interests equally, an impossible task in the given situation. At some stage, that

solicitor would have to advise one of the parties that they are best advised to get separate representation. Sometimes, in this and similar situations, the problem is resolved by both parties being advised by two different solicitors working in the same practice.

So how do you go about choosing one who will take care of your exclusive conveyancing interests in selling or buying a property? The *Golden Pages* or the *Yellow Pages* and *Independent Directory* (www.independentdirectory.ie) immediately come to mind. The Internet could be another source. Also a newspaper's business directory. Even the ordinary telephone directory might point a person to a solicitor who practices conveyancing in your particular area. Without thinking too hard about it, there is also the reliable walk down the street, to peer into the window or door or even to go in and ask the receptionist in a solicitor's office if there is a solicitor in the office 'who does conveyancing,' as is the most likely format of the question that will be posed. A 'yes' might result in an appointment being made with the conveyancing solicitor. A 'no' will result in the person walking away and trying to find one elsewhere.

Usually, families engage the same solicitor to look after the needs of all. That is fine. The solicitor gets to know the individual members, and they get to know the solicitor or solicitors in the practice. A special relationship and trust develops between them and each is happy to continue with this arrangement in perpetuity. There are many such arrangements as this throughout the country. However, everybody is not so conveniently looked after and must "shop around", not just to find a solicitor who is prepared to handle their conveyancing but one who is prepared to do it for a competitive price. The Law Society would also respond to a call, offering the name of a number of solicitors in a given area. The Law Society also has a search facility of solicitors on their website (www.lawsociety.ie) which people can go through themselves.

Despite all of this, a **personal recommendation** still remains one of the best ways to find the solicitor who is 'right' for a particular client. Walking in as a stranger off the street may well be fine for some people but, generally, if a friend, relative, colleague or your estate agent offers the name of 'a good solicitor,' then such advice is usually worth taking. Telephoning solicitors' offices, getting names, possibly speaking with a solicitor may sound easy, but it is not the ideal way of engaging the person who will become your closest and most vital agent during the crucial weeks ahead. Shopping around, getting a list of names of conveyancing solicitors, making direct contact with them and then finding out the fees that will be charged for your transaction is a tiresome business.

While the level of fees you will be faced with is crucial in your overall budget, just because one solicitor charges less fees than another should not be the sole yardstick by which you engage one. As in many spheres, cheapest is not always best. There are other issues that need to be factored into the equation, such as the area where you live and/or where the property you are selling is or the property that you want to buy is located, depending on whether you are a seller or a buyer. **Time and distance** can be of paramount importance for either a buyer or a seller. In one situation, the conveyancing solicitor may be located many miles away but because of the existence of good methods of communication today, the documents that need to pass between solicitor and client does not require that they are living and working in close proximity. In any event, time may not be of the essence in the transaction.

However, if a person needs the transaction to be concluded much quicker or perhaps it is a complex conveyance and requires more than the usual contact between solicitor and client, it **may** be more beneficial if the solicitor chosen has a practice relatively near where you are living or working. If you are a nuisance, however, your solicitor will not thank you for too much **unnecessary**

interference. If it happens that you do not hear from your solicitor more frequently than you expected, it does not mean that you and your transaction have been forgotten or shelved. But, in saying this, people should not hesitate to call on their solicitor from time to time for a progress report. They are entitled to it because they are paying for the service.

THE SOLICITOR'S DUTY OF CARE

As with other professionals providing a service in return for a fee, there is a contract between the seller and solicitor or between the buyer and solicitor. The solicitor owes a duty of care to the client. If the solicitor breaches that duty of care and the client suffers damage as a result, then the solicitor may be sued for professional negligence. All solicitors, like all doctors, like all barristers and other professionals, must take out expensive **professional indemnity insurance** to cover them in the event of them being successfully sued for negligence by clients, or in the case of doctors, by their patients.

But what is the standard of care that the law imposes on a solicitor in dealings with a client, whether a vendor or a purchaser? According to principles laid down in a Supreme Court judgment in an appeal decided in the mid-1980s:

> "The general duty owed by a solicitor to his client is to show him the degree of care to be expected in the circumstances from a reasonably careful and skilful solicitor. Usually, the solicitor will be held to have discharged that duty if he follows a practice common among the members of his profession… Conformity with the widely-accepted practice of his colleagues will normally rebut an allegation of negligence against a professional man, for the degree of care which the law expects of him is no higher than that to be expected from an ordinary reasonable member of the profession or of the speciality in question."

In other words, a solicitor holding himself or herself out as a specialist in conveyancing will be simply judged according to the degree of care expected from a solicitor with the conveyancing speciality. Practicing as a **conveyancer carries a heavy responsibility** for the solicitor. A failure to carry out a particular search of a property being purchased could have disastrous consequences for the purchaser, as one solicitor found to his cost as a result of a High Court case brought against him by his former client. The buyer thought he was buying a commercial property, which would (not 'could') be used as a registered hotel or guesthouse. However, a search of the Bord Fáilte Register at the time would have revealed that it could not have been, as it could not comply with the regulations then existing for such properties. Unfortunately, the search was not carried out and the premises turned out to be something of a white elephant with a consequent financial loss to the buyer.

TIME CONSUMING

Conveyancing is a time-consuming and tedious process. Because of all the questions that must be responded to by the opposing solicitor and as a result of the **searches** that must be made, it may take two or even three months to satisfactorily complete the transfer of good title. It cannot be rushed in the sense of sending a few hurried questions about the title to the other solicitor and ordering a few legal searches to be carried out in the **Registry of Deeds** or **Land Registry**…all done and dusted in a few days. If that were the case, the High Court lists would be swollen by the addition of many professional negligence cases. Conveyancing involves a lot of concentrated work, out of the sight of the client.

Once an offer has been made, or accepted, as the case may be, on a property, and both parties involved in the transaction have exchanged details of their respective solicitors - much like two parties involved in a traffic accident exchange the names of their insurance companies

- the solicitor's work then begins in earnest. Of course, the solicitors for the parties may have been involved in an advisory capacity from the very beginning, including in the case of an auction or in the tendering process. Buyers and sellers often think the rest is a doddle, merely a matter of tying up a few loose ends, like exchanging and then reading through a number of documents that make up the title to the property and then closing.

Later we will look in detail at what actually happens from this stage on, but it may help readers to know in a general way the kind of work their solicitor will be doing for their fee:

- Checking the background of the property involved in the transaction and having **searches or investigations** carried out with, among others, the local authority, and the various offices where titles are registered and, crucially, charges (debts) are registered against property.

- Minutely examining the legality of contracts and leases for property that is **leasehold** (which will be explained later) and identifying, and dealing with, any problems that might arise.

- Investigating the actual title to the property.

- Drawing up the contract and ensuring that all the necessary legalities are observed.

- Dealing with any post-contract problems that might arise.

- Arranging the closing and last minute pre-closing searches.

- Post-closing obligations such as registering the buyer's ownership.

HOW MUCH WILL IT COST?

The first thing that a buyer or seller will usually want to know is what the solicitor will charge. What are the legal fees? What will be the Government's cut out of the transaction in terms of stamp duty and Value Added Tax? We will presume that Capital Gains Tax is not payable on the transactions we are discussing in this book because the buyer is not buying a second home as an investment, and the seller is disposing of their family home as a prelude to buying another property to reside in. The legal costs will be discussed in the next chapter.

Chapter 8

LEGAL COSTS

In the last chapter the task of finding a solicitor for buyers and sellers of property was discussed. When you were making your inquiries - telephoning, asking family, friends and colleagues and generally shopping around - to secure the services of a solicitor you felt you were satisfied with, fees would not normally have been at the forefront of your mind.

In fact, while legal fees are a very important consideration, money as such, should not be the sole criteria in deciding which individual solicitor or firm of solicitors should be engaged. Other things are also important, such as how you get on with the person, would that solicitor be available for direct contact from day to day, did the solicitor take the time to put you at your ease and explain simply what was involved in the process or did they seem in a hurry and ushered you out of the office as though you were an irritant or nuisance? All of these questions are important in their own way, but there is no hiding the fact that the legal costs will concentrate the mind, once the first contact is made with members of the legal profession.

The collective public mind has been 'conditioned' to the fact that all lawyers earn mega fees. Some do but the majority do not. The perception that all lawyers charge what the average person would consider to be staggering fees, stems from media reports and comments of the fees paid by the State to lawyers working in the various tribunals of inquiry that have taken place since the early 1990s, starting with the Beef Tribunal.

Most of that type of information was revealed in Dáil Éireann in response to parliamentary questions. However, only a small coterie of lawyers has earned a million or more Euro in fees out of their work for the tribunals. They should not be used as a yardstick to measure what the average solicitor or barrister earns. By any stretch of the imagination, the conveyancing fees involved in the average sale or purchase will be very modest. In fact, considering the amount of work involved, including the time spent checking the smallest detail, preparing contracts and other documents, ordering or carrying out legal searches and taking care of many other details too numerous to chronicle here, many a skilled tradesperson would shy away in today's expensive climate if offered the same fee for comparable labour time.

FEES AND DISBURSEMENTS

The first thing that must be said is that solicitors structure their charges in different ways. Some charge a fixed fee, while others charge on the basis of a percentage of the value the property was sold at or purchased - depending on which party they are acting for. Because of the high cost of houses and apartments in today's market, any solicitor charging on the basis of a percentage of the value, would reap very handsome rewards. In some situations, the charging of such a fee would be a step too far for some people, especially if it is a second-hand property on which stamp duty is payable. As a result, solicitors are amenable to charging a fixed or flat fee for their conveyancing services. Accordingly, when people meet a solicitor for the first time and they are considering engaging the solicitor, they should put shyness or hesitancy or fear or any such feelings aside and **ask the hard question** straight up: what will you charge?

PROFESSIONAL FEE

What many people forget when they are asking or talking about what the solicitor is charging is that the fee being charged is just that. It is the **professional fee only**. This can vary from solicitor to solicitor and from firm to firm. It may be a fixed charge or a percentage of the value of the property. It is the fee the solicitor is charging for his or her time and expertise in doing the work. It does not include other charges known as **'disbursements'** or **'outlay'** which can account for a considerable, and usually greater, amount of the total legal bill presented to the client for payment in the days and after the closing or just before.

CHECKLIST

In order to reduce or eliminate unpleasant surprises, or even shock, later when the solicitor's invoice is received in the post, there are a number of questions a prospective client should put to the solicitor at their initial meeting. One of the first questions should be:

- Are you charging on the basis of a **flat or fixed fee** or on a **percentage**?

- If it is a flat or fixed fee, what is your **professional fee**?

- If the solicitor is charging by percentage, what roughly will that amount to?

- What is the estimated total of the **other legal costs called 'disbursements'**?

In addition, Value Added Tax **(VAT)** at the current rate of **21%** will be charged on the solicitor's professional fee. This is the first 'take' by the Revenue on behalf of the Government from your transaction. The second will be stamp duty, if it applies to a particular transaction.

- The word 'disbursements' covers just about everything else a solicitor will charge. It may also be called 'outlay' and includes such charges as the stamp duty, if appropriate. This will usually be several thousands of Euros and total many multiples of the highest professional fee a solicitor can charge for his or her own services in the case of a second-hand house. Of course, what angers many purchasers of second-hand properties faced with a big stamp duty bill is that they see nothing for their money, unlike in the case of the fees charged by their solicitor, by other professionals such as surveyors, engineers or architects, legal searchers, cost accountants or by tradesmen such as electricians or plumbers brought in to check or repair some aspects of the property. The disbursements or outlay can also include the cost of engaging a specialist to carry out various **searches** (at a cost of about €90 for each search), transferring the mortgage money from the lender to the account of the person selling their home – in the case of a second-hand property – the secretarial costs, photocopying, telephone, fax, postage. In addition, when representing a purchaser, the solicitor's disbursements or outlay will include the cost of registering the name of the new owner in the Land Registry.

- In summary, it can be seen that there is no set fee for legal fees. Market forces dictate what they will be in any given case. Solicitors practice in a competitive field, and people shopping round for a solicitor are best advised to bluntly ask at the outset what the professional fee and likely outlay are going to be. Buyers and sellers must remember that the professional fee is only part of the legal costs they will be faced with paying after the keys of the house or apartment are handed to them, in the case of a buyer, or by them, if they are sellers. Usually, buyers have just moved in to their new home – which, of course, may be second-hand – when the solicitor's bill comes in through the letter box and is a **stark reminder** of the heavy financial undertaking they have on their hands, not to mention the first mortgage repayment that must be met about four weeks later.

- For first-time buyers, who are responsible for almost half the new homes purchased in Ireland each year, this is usually a time for tightening the belt until the legal bills, at least, are discharged. According to a study last year, more than one-quarter (28%) of them spend between 31% and 40% of their take-home pay on their mortgage alone, while one-third said it was between 21% and 30%. These statistics and comments may seem out of place here but they are included in order to place in context the actuality of become the proud owner of a new home. It comes at a substantial cost.

ACTUAL FEES

So what is your solicitor likely to charge, whether as a fixed or flat fee or on a percentage. While solicitors traditionally charged 1% of the purchase price as their professional fee, in general terms, a solicitor today may charge between 0.75% and 1.0% of the purchase price or about €1,000 as a flat fee in the case of a buyer and on a similar basis for the person selling a house or apartment. That fee of €1,000 is considerably less than what it used to be as a flat fee. £1,000 was more likely the order of the day five or six years ago. Some firms of solicitors have advertised their fees to be €999, but potential clients should first clarify with them if these fixed or flat fees are professional fees only and are not inclusive of disbursements or outlay, which they do not appear to be as it would be impossible to put an exact figure at the outset on what the disbursements in any one case will be. In fact, outlay could put another €500 on top of the professional fee in the case of a new house purchase.

One such firm which advertised its conveyancing services at a fixed rate fee of €999 plus VAT and outlay, is Pierse & Fitzgibbon solicitors, based in Listowel, Co. Kerry, who offer their legal services under the style or title of **'Home Buy, Home Sell.'** One of the principals, Robert Pierse said this fee was geared especially towards members of **Credit Unions** who were buying or selling. He said the majority of conveyancing services cost 1% of a house's sale price plus €127 plus VAT plus outlay and, as charges were not fixed, this could often lead to considerable costs for buyers and sellers. On that basis, the following gives an indication of what the professional fee would be if it was based on 1% of the price:

- €100,000... €1,127 plus VAT plus outlay.
- €150,000... €1,627 " VAT   "   "
- €200,000... €2,127 " VAT   "   "

There are few houses in Dublin and elsewhere, which can be purchased or sold for €200,000. The smallest new house in a development will usually fetch more than €300,000. It can be seen, therefore, that a buyer or seller would save considerably if they find a solicitor who charges a flat professional fee of €999 or €1,000, even though at the beginning they might be shocked when they heard that they might be faced with having to pay such a fee.

One or more of the building societies have arranged deals with solicitors for their mortgage borrowers, under which the borrower will be charged a flat fee of €985 plus VAT and outlay, irrespective of the value of the property. There may be others who charge less by way of a special price in return for securing the mortgage business of the potential borrower.

- With the average cost of a home sale being €300,000 today, a seller or buyer charged a flat fee is faring much better than one being charged at a minimum of 0.75% of the value of the property, even without the VAT and outlay being included. In return for using their services to get a mortgage from one of a number of stated number of banks and building societies, one firm in the Irish market promised that borrowers would only have to pay €675 (plus VAT and outlay). It is a competitive market and it will pay borrowers to shop around to get the best deals from solicitors (and from estate agents). The consumer finance website, www.askaboutmoney.ie, is another source that may be worth checking in this regard. However, despite the promise of 'cheap' legal fees (i.e. professional fee plus VAT plus outlay), borrowers should exercise extreme caution and not accept any offer without first finding out exactly what they are expected to 'give' in return.

LIKELY OUTLAY

The items that are likely to appear as disbursements or outlay fees and charges in the invoice sent out by the solicitor in the case of a property purchase are:

- Stamp duty.

- Memorial.

- Assignment of life policy.

- Land Registration fees.

- Land Certificate.

- Copy Instrument.

- Copy folio.

- Miscellaneous including marriage/death certificate, commissioner for oaths, searches and other petty outlay.

- Postage, telephone and photocopying.

- VAT at 21%.

OTHER CHECKS

The solicitor has to make many checks and carry out legal searches from the start until the very end of the process. These would include checking if the property is exempt from stamp duty. If the solicitor is acting for the seller of a second-hand property, the owner, which might happen to be a charity, should be exempt from having to pay **Capital Gains Tax** or **Stamp Duty**. It may also be necessary to see if there is some debt or other charge registered against the property.

It would not be unusual for a problem of some sort or other to arise before completion. Take the situation where the closing date agreed between the parties passes without the purchaser coming up with the balance of the purchase money and completing. If that happens, the solicitor for the seller may serve a notice on the defaulting party calling on them to complete by a certain date, and warning that if they fail to comply with the terms of the notice within a specified period, they would be deemed to have failed to comply with the contract. The innocent party, as such, would be free to pursue the defaulting party – a buyer - and might call on them to pay interest to the seller on the balance of the purchase money unpaid, from the date of the agreed closing date to the date of the actual completion of the sale. This type of problem could arise where a purchaser had difficulty in getting mortgage approval. It also arises where completion of the purchase is contingent on the buyer selling their own property…the dreaded chain effect.

On the other hand, there may also be a problem from the seller's perspective, relating to the fact that the house being sold is in the sole name of, say, the husband. The reason that the Family Home Protection Act came into force in 1976 was to protect the interests of the spouse whose name was not on the title deeds. It may be that the husband was trying to sell the house without his wife's knowledge. While this should be clarified by the buyer's solicitor at the **Requisitions on Title** stage, it could mean a delay, for no other reason than the solicitor will require the non-disposing spouse, i.e. the wife, to complete a standard declaration consenting to the sale. Perhaps the spouse is not available and delay ensues. The protection is given in section 3, subsection (1) of the 1976 Act, which states:

> 'Where a spouse without the prior consent in writing of the other spouse, purports to convey any interest in the family home to any person except the other spouse, then subject to subsections (2) and (3) and section 4, the purported conveyance shall be void.'

There is great potential for delay, and possibly court applications where serious problems arise. It requires vigilance on the part of the solicitors acting for both parties to ensure that the rights of all parties are respected.

Chapter 9

GETTING AND GIVING GOOD TITLE

When a solicitor acts for a purchaser of residential property, he or she will also act on behalf of the financial institution providing the mortgage for the purchaser in carrying out an investigating into the title to the property. This is now standard practice and certainly gives impetus to a process that could - and used to - be delayed for long periods because of the volume of pressure on the lenders' own in-house or contracted outside conveyancer(s). This is one reason why lenders will not accept conveyancing done by anybody other than by a solicitor. This has to be seen in the context of the state of Irish land law which is badly in need of reform. How a lay person could properly investigate a title and spot a problem rooted in antiquated land law, contract law and landlord and tenant law which might possibly have to be brought to court for resolution, would seem to be beyond the knowledge of a non-legal person.

CERTIFICATE OF TITLE

Lenders now allow the purchaser's solicitor to take responsibility for having the mortgage duly executed by the borrowers, stamping and registering the borrower's title and providing a certificate of title to the lending institution. This practice was adopted as a result of public pressure on lenders, especially building societies, as buyers had to pay not only their own solicitor on the purchase of the property but also pay the building society's solicitor who had independently investigated the title to the property being purchased. This was very unfair and added, what many viewed, as an unnecessary expense to the already heavy financial burden carried by buyers.

There was strong public discontent over a practice where buyers felt they were being unduly penalised by lenders who were making thousands of pounds profit off the backs of each of their borrowers in repaying the mortgage over its full life. The purpose in introducing the new certificate of title procedure was to save the buyer the expense of having to pay fees to two solicitors for doing what was essentially the same work. So the new arrangement with the Law Society was indeed a welcome development that buyers in today's market get the benefit of.

BUYING ABROAD

As referred to earlier, there is always a chance of a conflict of interest where the seller and buyer agree to engage the same solicitor for the transaction. The public must be aware of this potential for conflict, which could cause either party considerable financial loss, at the very least. While this is important here in Ireland, it is even more imperative when Irish people are buying a house or apartment in Spain, France, Hungary, Bulgaria or wherever. The temptation to agree to the suggestion of the developer's sales representatives to use their own local lawyer, allegedly at a cost and convenience saving, could end up costing the buyer considerably more, not only in financial terms but frustration because of delay in reaching the closing and an absence of information about how the purchase is progressing.

How can an Irish resident possibly 'police' a transaction being conducted in a different country, while having no knowledge of local laws and while dealing with people with a few words of English or no English or an agent who doesn't respond to telephone calls from Ireland? The pace of progress in getting things done can be astonishingly slow in continental countries especially. Generally, the road to buying a place in the sun can be strewn with landmines, according to the experience of many Irish people.

However, the chances of any of those landmines exploding is minimised or eliminated if potential buyers engage their own solicitor in Ireland to take care of the transaction abroad.

Most firms of solicitors in Ireland use agents in other countries to deal with their Irish clients' business in that foreign country, in the same way as country solicitors use town agents to transact their business in the Four Courts, Dublin. They will nominate a local firm to transact the business. Some firms advertise their expertise at taking care of property transactions abroad. As the case with finding a solicitor to transact the normal property transfer in Ireland, reputation and the necessity to shop around are the best ways of finding the one that suits your needs.

ROOTS OF TITLE

In a transaction for the purchase or sale of a house or apartment, what the owner in each case is doing is disposing or acquiring a particular title to the particular property, whatever the case may be. Getting good title depends on the quality of the root of title being offered. When conveyancers speak of the root of title, they mean the important document from which the seller or vendor intends to demonstrate that the title to the property starts from. The remainder of the title remains rooted in that first document.

The type of the particular title in each case will vary to include short and long leaseholds, fee farm grants which involves the conveyance of a fee simple subject to the payment of a perpetual rent to the grantor and his successors in title, life estates, leases for lives renewable forever, and other strange sounding interests, which only solicitors and barristers, legal academics and students of land and conveyancing law will know and recognise for the kind of interest they give in a particular property. To the uninitiated, it is a boring subject but is absolutely vital for the conveyancer to know, as he or she must ensure that good marketable title is either being disposed of or acquired.

LEASEHOLD INTEREST

The difference between freehold property and leasehold property is vital. When the time comes to buy, sell or lease property, it will be vital for the client and their solicitor to know what type of interest in the particular property is involved. Estates in land fall into two categories, **freehold** and **leasehold** estates. They are two very different concepts.

Leasehold is a normal contractual arrangement which must contain all the necessary ingredients of a valid contract to enable the property transaction to be legally valid. There are, in fact, several types of leasehold estate, which are classified into four main categories:

- A leasehold estate that is granted for **a certain term.** This type is common in this country Ireland with very long terms of years e.g. **999** years and **10,000 years**. (In commercial property transactions where a company is leasing an office block, the terms would be much shorter, say for 25 years, with review periods every few years and possibly with an option for the tenant to buy the property outright at the end of the period of the tenancy period). A vigilant conveyancer must establish how many of the 999 years of the lease, for example, remain before the lease is determined or ended. Legally, the purchaser of a leasehold property is merely a tenant of the party who granted the lease or his successors. However, because of the long number of years that the lease has to run, the reality usually is that the purchaser will hold the property for not merely his or her own lifetime, but also that of many succeeding generations. Apartments, so many of which are being released onto the market today, are usually leasehold.

- A second category of leasehold estate is **a periodic tenancy** This is also a fixed term tenancy with a minimum period, of one week or one month which will continue for successive periods until either party to the agreement determines the tenancy according to its terms.

- The third category is a **tenancy at will**. This tenancy may continue indefinitely, but can be determined by either party at any time. Because of this, the tenant's tenure is uncertain and insecure.

- The fourth category of leasehold estate or, more correctly, interest, is a **tenancy at sufferance**. It arises where a tenant fails to quit or leave the premises at the natural end of the tenancy, but remains on or 'holds over' without the landlord's agreement. The only reason that he is not classed as a trespasser is because his entry onto the premises was lawful at the beginning of the tenancy. The tenant therefore remains on at the landlord's sufferance.

FREEHOLD INTEREST

There are three main types: **fee simple, fee tail** and **life estate**.

- The **fee simple** is the largest estate and is the nearest to absolute ownership. The reason that it is not quite absolute is because of the theory of tenure under which the State could take over the property, as where the present owner of the property dies without making a will (i.e. intestate) and there is nobody left to take it over. The State may become owner in those circumstances. However, this rarely happens.

- The **fee tail** is a lesser estate in property. It is a relic of an era when land was regarded as the most secure source of wealth.

- The **life estate** is an estate that lasts for the duration of someone's life only.

A book could be written about each and every category of freehold and leasehold interest, such is the complexity and history of these very important interests under which property has been, or is being, held in Ireland.

REGISTERED AND UNREGISTERED LAND

Another area that the client's solicitor will be concerned with on behalf of the house purchaser, especially, is the question whether the dwelling is on **registered** or **unregistered** land. The type of deed that will be drafted by the solicitor in the particular transaction will depend on whether the land is registered or unregistered. Registration is made of the ownership of an estate or interest in the land. While one interest may be registered in the **Land Registry**, the title to another estate or interest in the same land may be unregistered. Registered land is registered in the Land Registry and there are two systems of registration – **registration of deeds**, and **registration of title**.

Registration of title to property is regulated by the **Registration of Title Act 1964** and several sets of rules, and is operated by the Land Registry. When the transaction on behalf of the purchaser is completed, the solicitor will register the client's ownership of the property in the Land Registry and pay the appropriate fee, which will be included in the solicitor's invoice. A **register of title** is a list of owners of land, with details of the property and of the charges and restrictions affecting it. The legislation states that registration is conclusive evidence of the owner's title. It also provides for the description of property, not only by reference to a written record of the title called a folio, but also by reference to a map kept by the Land Registry. The solicitor must ensure that the description of the property in the title deeds is the same as that in the contract for sale. The essence of registration is that it protects the interests of a person who legally acquires an interest in property.

FEES

There are fees payable to the Land Registry for the transfer of the property deeds into the name of its new owner. These fees or charges are payable up front to the solicitor before the closing. This is in compliance with the undertaking (see below) the solicitor gave to the lending institution in taking up the title documents. The wording of the undertaking stipulates that the solicitor is in funds to register the title.

The amount of the registration fees alone that the purchaser will have to pay to the solicitor to enable this transaction to be carried out will depend on the purchase price of the property. However, intending purchasers should **budget for between €700 and €1,000** for Land Registry registration fees. For the registration of a house valued between €255,001 and €385,001, the registration fee is €500. For any property valued above that, the registration fee is €625. The fee for registering property of lower value is considerably less, starting at €125, which is the lowest on the scale of registration fees. In addition to that, the mortgage must be registered in the Land Registry against the property. That costs another €125.

These fees are expensive compared with the cost of registering a deed of assignment or conveyance in the Registry of Deeds, which is €44. Searches in the latter need only go back 20 years, unlike the Land Registry where lending institutions require conveyancing solicitors to search back for 40 years. However, greatly assisting searchers today is the fact that it is on-line searches which considerably speeds up the process. Some solicitors will pay these registration fees at the time of registration and will recoup their outlay as part of their final invoice to the client. Others will seek get payment for this outlay up-front from the client.

Any document relating to land may be registered in the **Registry of Deeds**, which is situated beside the King's Inns, in Henrietta Street, Dublin 1. Registration gives some security to purchasers and mortgagees (i.e. mortgage lenders such as building societies; the borrower is known as the mortgagor) as to the existence only of a certain document. Searches are carried out in the Registry of Deeds right up to completion to ensure that no document has been omitted from the title.

INVESTIGATION OF TITLE

The post-contractual stage of the conveyancing process is referred to as the investigation of title. When the contract for sale is entered into, the seller or vendor is obliged to prove that he or she can transfer the property to the buyer, although this process can start much earlier if the solicitor for the vendor gives some of the title documents to the purchaser's solicitor for examination.

OBJECTIONS AND REQUISITIONS ON TITLE

A vital part of the conveyancing solicitor's duty is to raise questions with the solicitor for the other party about the property at the centre of the process. They cover an extremely wide range of issues, including reminding the vendor to do various things before completion. Every question posed must be specific. The following is a sample of the **44 questions** provided for in the standard form of the objections and requisitions on title (2001 edition) provided by the Law Society for use by its members:

- Is the property subject to any right-of-way, water, light, air or drainage or to any other easement or turbary right or other *profit à prendre* or any reservation, covenant, condition or restriction or to any right of any kind?

- Which of the boundaries belong to the property and which are party boundaries?

- Is the property registered under the **National House Building Guarantee Scheme/HomeBond Scheme**?

- Have the services (including roads, lanes, footpaths,

sewers and drains) abutting or servicing the property been taken over by the Local Authority?

- Confirm that clear vacant possession will be handed over at closing.

- Is the property or any part of it let? If so, furnish now the Lease or Tenancy Agreement.

- Is the property subject to any mortgage or charge? If so, give full particulars.

- If it is a newly erected property, furnish immediately a list of documents, including draft site map, draft indemnity in relation to defects, floor area certificate, and at closing hand over documents, including a completed memorial and HB 10 Agreement under the **HomeBond Scheme** completed by the vendor.

- If the property or any part of it is a 'family home' as defined in the Family Home Protection Act 1976, the Family Law Act 1995 and Family Law (Divorce) Act 1996, furnish the prior written consent of the vendor's spouse, and verify the marriage by statutory declaration exhibiting a copy of the civil marriage certificate and draft declaration and copy of the exhibit for approval.

- Has there been in relation to the property any development (including change of use or exempted development) within the meaning of the Local Government (Planning and Development) Act 1963 on or after October 1, 1964? In respect of all such developments furnish a number of documents, including grant of planning permission or outline planning permission, building bye-law approval, certificate of an engineer/architect of conformity with the permission/approval (if applicable) and that all conditions other than financial conditions have been complied with.

The requisitions are numerous and detailed and require

considerable work by the vendor's solicitor to comply with the various requests, right up to and including the day the closing takes place. A perusal of the full list reveals that many would not apply to the sale of a private dwelling as they relate to such things as commercial property, agricultural land and even milk quotas. Nevertheless they all at least require to be read and to be responded to.

SOLICITORS' UNDERTAKINGS

One of the gravest obligations that a solicitor must comply with is known as a solicitor's undertaking. The solicitor can give it personally, or it can be given by the solicitor on behalf of a client as the agent for that client. It would arise most often in the area of conveyancing, e.g. the purchaser's solicitor would give a written undertaking to take up the title documents being held by a lender and to hold them in trust for the lender while they are in his or her possession, and to ensure that the borrower gets good marketable title to the property. Failure to comply with an undertaking leaves a solicitor open to a charge of misconduct before the disciplinary committee of the Law Society on a complaint by an aggrieved party.

POWER OF ATTORNEY

Another function of the solicitor will be to get power of attorney from the client, say the borrower, to carry out a number of transactions on his or her behalf, for example, to perfect and register the deed of mortgage/charge in favour of the lending institution, which provided the mortgage to the solicitor's client.

Chapter 10

STAMP DUTY

Nobody, but nobody, likes paying stamp duty. It is 'dead' money, as the saying goes. Payment of a sum of money that will run into several thousands of Euros at the end of a property transaction is the last thing a buyer wants. It is a duty on documents that are used in the transfer of property. It is not part of the professional fee charged by the solicitor, but will appear in the list of disbursements or outlay supplied at the close of transaction.

No matter how gently the solicitor's letter is worded a claim for a sum of several thousand Euro, it usually comes as a shock to the system because the solicitor's own fee plus the VAT and outlaw will be considerable less than the stamp duty charge itself. However, while first-time buyers can now escape having to pay it if they fulfil certain rigid conditions in buying new or second-hand properties, the reality is that it still applies to the transfer of most second-hand properties and remains an unwelcome burden, despite the fact that reduced rates now apply to purchases up to €635,000, well above the average price of a second-hand house which has been calculated at €400,000. The full rate of 9% still applies to second-hand properties over the €635,000 threshold.

While the ordinary buyer will have no choice but to pay the stamp duty as a separate visible transaction, the public has a mistaken perception that it can be included as part of the purchase price and possibly concealed in the mortgage by a co-operative estate agent or solicitor. The public might also think that a buyer of a second-hand property with a value right on, or just above, the **threshold for stamp duty** could escape liability for stamp duty by paying the total legal fees of the vendor. Such a move would bring the purchase price below the level of €317,500 and result in the buyer escaping having the pay stamp duty as such. Probably. However, a potential buyer contemplating such a move would be well advised to get legal advice from his or her solicitor before putting down a deposit, although it would appear to be a genuine way of evading stamp duty.

FIRST-TIME BUYERS

The main beneficiaries of the reduction in stamp duty rates are first-time buyers of second-hand houses and apartments. Because it is so difficult for people who qualify as first-time buyers to buy into the property market in the first place, the abolition of stamp duty in the case of the second-hand property market has considerably eased their financial burden. As a result of the threshold changes, they could save over €10,000. First-time buyers have been paying a national average of €303,148 for houses and €284,574 for apartments, according to figures released with the December **2004 Budget**. Consequently, first-time buyers will save the very considerable sum of €11,368 in stamp duty savings by buying the averaged price second-hand house, or €10,671 in buying an apartment.

The most common charge to stamp duty affecting individuals is the stamp duty on the purchase of residential houses and apartments. The amount payable depends on:

• The price paid (or the market value where the price paid is less than the market value of the property).

• Whether the property is new or second-hand, and

• whether the purchaser is a first-time buyer, owner-occupier or investor.

As can be seen, there is now considerable benefit available for first-time buyers. Nevertheless, to qualify for the exemption in the case of new properties, they must measure less than 125 square metres (1,345 square feet).

WHO QUALIFIES TO BE CATEGORISED AS A FIRST-TIME BUYER?

The Revenue defines a first-time buyer as a person who has not previously bought or built a house in this country or abroad, and who is purchasing a house or apartment for use as their principal place of residence. Where there is more than one buyer – such as a couple buying jointly or in common – each of the buyers must be a first-time buyer to qualify to get the reduced first-time buyer rate.

The rates of duty for first-time buyers have been reduced for deeds of conveyance or transfers executed on or after December 2, 2004. The rates applicable for residential property (whether new or second-hand) are as follows:

Aggregate Consideration	First-time Buyer Rate pre December 2, 2004 Rate	First-time Buyers Rate	Full rate
Less than €127,000	Exempt	Exempt	Exempt
€127,001-€190,000	Exempt	Exempt	3%
€190,501-€254,000	3%	Exempt	4%
€254,001-€317,500	3.75%	Exempt	5%
€317,501-€381,000	4.5%	3%	6%
€381,001-€635,000	7.5%	6%	7.5%
Over €635,000	9%	9%	9%

According to the Revenue, these rates apply to the entire consideration or value of the property, e.g.:

- Where the consideration for a property is €150,000 (and the purchaser is not a first-time buyer), the stamp duty liability would be €4,500 (€150,000 @ 3%).

- Where the consideration for a property is €350,000 (and the purchaser is not a first-time buyer), the stamp duty liability would be €21,000 (€350,000 @ 6%).

- Where the consideration for a property is €350,000 and the purchaser is a first-time buyer (where the deed of conveyance is executed on or after the 2nd December, 2004), the stamp duty would be €10,500 (€350,000 @ 3%).

AREA OF HOUSE/APARTMENT

The Revenue applies a very strict rule regarding the size of a house or apartment that qualifies for an exemption from having to pay stamp duty. The limit is 125 square metres (about 1,346 sq. ft.). The house or apartment **must not exceed a total floor area of 125 sq.metres**. This applies to all owner-occupiers, including first-time buyers. To prove that there has been compliance with this requirement, a certificate of compliance issued by the Department of the Environment and Local Government has to be provided. The purchaser's solicitor will look for this floor area compliance certificate from the seller as part of the requisitions discussed in the previous chapter. If there is a breach of the requirement, the Revenue will seek a clawback of the of the stamp duty from the buyer.

Owner occupiers, including first-time buyers, of new houses and apartments where the total floor area **exceeds 125 sq. metres** are charged with stamp duty at the appropriate residential property rate (see table above), on the site value (excluding VAT), or one-quarter of the total value of the house including the site (excluding VAT), which ever is the greater. The size of the floor area must be certified by a qualified architect, engineer or surveyor. Again, there is a clawback to the Revenue of the stamp duty in the event of a breach.

A clawback will also arise if rent is obtained from the letting of the house or apartment for a period of **five-years** from the date of the conveyance or transfer, other than under the **rent-a-room** scheme. Under this scheme there is no clawback of the first-time buyer or owner occupier reliefs where rent is received by the person in occupation of the house or apartment, on or after April 6, 2001, for the letting of furnished accommodation in part of the house or apartment.

The clawback amounts to the difference between the higher stamp duty rate and the duty paid, and it becomes payable on the date that rent is first received from the property. However, it should be noted that a clawback will not arise where the property is sold to an unrelated third party during the five-year period.

STAMP DUTY ON SITES

A person contemplating getting a site and building a house to their own design needs to be aware of the stamp duty rates that might be applicable. The reliefs referred to above may, and will, come into play in certain circumstances. The rules as outlined by the Revenue in this regard are:

- Where an individual purchases a site in connection with, or as part of, an agreement to build a house or apartment on that site, then stamp duty will be charged, subject to the reliefs referred to above, based on the aggregate amount of the site cost and the building costs at the appropriate residential property rate.

- The transfer of a site from a parent to a child is exempt from stamp duty where the site transfer is for the purpose of constructing a house which will be the child's main residence and where the value of the site does not exceed €254,000.

Much of the above information was gleaned from the Revenue's own website at www.revenue.ie, which is very consumer-friendly and extremely informative. Buyers are well advised to check it out for themselves when planning a purchase, or a sale in the event of a capital gains tax or other tax exposure.

AFFORDABLE HOUSING

In an urban area like Dublin where property values continue to spiral, many young people find it impossible to buy a new house or apartment in the private sector, despite having what are generally regarded as good incomes each week. As a result, there has been an exodus into towns within a two-hour commuting distance of the capital where property values come within their reach.

However, there is another route that young people are, and should, considering taking to get onto the property ladder without having to travel very far from their city base. This is called the affordable housing scheme. It has become so popular that applicants for housing in the inner city of Dublin have to endure the trauma of taking part in a lottery and hoping their names will be picked out.

A typical advertisement relating to affordable housing was posted in the daily newspapers earlier this year by **South Dublin County Council**. It asked:

- Are you having difficulty in purchasing property?

- Do you feel priced out of the market?

- Do you need an affordable home in the South Dublin County Council area?

The advert went on the state a number of conditions, including that applicants must be first-time buyers, their **gross income must be under €36,800** in the previous tax year, and they must be currently employed for a minimum of six months or self-employed for at least a year. Any person wishing to be considered was invited to submit an application for one of the two or three bedroom houses the council was disposing at various locations throughout the county. This was a very attractive offer and one that would have been welcomed by very many people.

According to the **Department of the Environment, Heritage and Local Government**, the Affordable Housing Scheme provides for the building of new houses in areas where house prices have created an affordable gap for lower income house purchasers. The houses would be offered for sale to eligible first-time purchasers **at cost price,** and at a significant discount from the market value of comparable houses in the area.

If a house purchased under the affordable housing scheme is **resold** within 10 years, the percentage of the sale price discounted by the local authority would be payable to the local authority by the purchaser on the proceeds of the re-sale of the house. The amount payable is reduced by 10% for each complete year after the 10th year (i.e. for the next 10 years, making it 20 years in total) during which the person who purchased the property has been in occupation as his or her normal place of residence.

INCOME TEST

The current income test is applied as follows:

Single-income household

- To ascertain if an applicant for a house under the scheme is eligible, multiply the gross income (before tax) in the last income year by 2.5. If the result is **€36,800** or less, the applicant is eligible under this criteria.

Two-income household

- Multiply the gross income (before tax) of the greater of the two incomes in the last income tax year by 2.5 and add to it the gross income of the lesser earner in the last income tax year. If the result is **€92,000** or less, the applicant was eligible.

INTEREST RATE

The current (as of February 14, 2005) interest rate available from the Department to successful applicants is 2.95% variable or a fixed rate for a period of 4.45% for five years. As in the case of every other loan, other than one with a fixed rate, interest rates are liable to vary, upwards or downwards, as financial markets fluctuate.

POPULAR SCHEME

The popularity of the affordable housing scheme, which is becoming more and more attractive to first-time buyers, can be gauged from the fact that the Department's target of completing 1,000 houses a year is being met. It operates throughout the entire country but is especially popular in Dublin. A spokesman for the Department said it was up to each local authority to initiate the scheme in their own functional area. By and large, if the authorities see a need for affordable houses, they would be produced.

Chapter 11

EUROPEAN PERSPECTIVES AND E-CONVEYANCING

Rare, indeed, is any area of life in Ireland that is not affected in one way or another by virtue of our membership of the European Union. Accession to the EEC more than 30 years ago brought its rewards and its obligations, and it continues to do so. In the near future, yet another obligation will be imposed on property owners, including sellers and lessors, to furnish buyers and lessees, respectively, with an energy performance certificate in respect of the building being sold or leased, as the case may be. **Energy savings** are the by-words of the new law.

The obligation on the sellers of houses (and apartment blocks) to furnish an energy performance certificate to buyers is not yet part of Irish law, but it must be so by January 4, 2006, the date on which Ireland is legally bound to transpose into Irish domestic law an EU Directive setting out the **energy performance of buildings**.

The EU law is known as the Energy Performance of Buildings Directive (2002/91/EC) and it was adopted on December 16, 2002. While the EU provided the deadline by which Member States were obliged to transpose the EU law into domestic law, the Directive has an in-built provision, which allows Member States a period of three further years from January 4, 2006 in which to transpose the **practical implementation** of the more complex provisions into their own domestic law. This extra period, which is discretionary to each Member State, is allowed "because of lack of qualified and/or accredited experts." These provisions concern:

- The energy performance certification 'labelling' of

newly constructed buildings and existing buildings (when existing buildings are sold or let).

- Improvement of the energy efficiency of boilers, and

- Inspection of air conditioning systems.

In December 2004, a proposed timetable for the implementation of the Directive in this country was put forward by **Sustainable Energy Ireland** on behalf of the Inter-Departmental Working Group. It was contained in a draft action plan presented to the **Minister for the Environment, Heritage and Local Government** before Christmas, and was due for publication for public and industry comment since then.

OBJECTIVE

The objective of the new law is to promote the improvement of the energy performance of buildings within the community, taking into account outdoor climatic and local conditions, as well as indoor requirements and cost-effectiveness. The Directive lays down requirements as regards:

- The general framework for a methodology of calculation of the integrated energy performance of **buildings**.

- The application of minimum requirements on the energy performance of **new buildings.**

- The application of minimum requirements on the energy performance of large existing buildings that are subject to **major renovation**.

- **Energy certification** of buildings.

- **Regular inspection** of boilers, and of air-conditioning systems in buildings.

- An assessment of the heating installation in which the boilers are **more than 15 years old**.

The first thought that comes to mind is that implementation of the new law will provide great opportunities for environmental and other suitably qualified engineers, plumbers, central heating, air conditioning and other specialists, in carrying out the necessary inspections and completing the certification. The devil is in the detail, as the old saying goes, and while it is unclear at this stage how the certification will be sought by a buyer's solicitor, in the case of a new or old house for example, it may be included as a new **Requisition on Title**, to add to the 44 already in existence.

If a buyer's solicitor requested the seller's solicitor to furnish such a certificate at the usual stage of the conveyancing process, it would probably require the seller engaging an expert to carry out the necessary energy checks and then furnishing the certificate. Alternatively, it could also involve a suitably qualified inspector from a local authority carrying out the checks and then certifying the building. Whatever methodology is finally adopted, it could add delay and additional expense to a conveyancing process for the seller but very valuable information and comfort for the buyer.

DEFINITIONS
According to the Directive:

- 'Energy performance of a building' is defined as the amount of energy actually consumed or estimated to meet the different needs associated with a standardised use of the building, which may include, among other things, heating, hot water heating, cooling, ventilation and lighting.

- 'Energy performance certificate of a building' is a certificate recognised by this country or a legal person designated by it.

- 'Combined heat and power (CHP)' is defined as the simultaneous conversion of primary fuels into mechanical or electrical and thermal energy, meeting certain quality criteria of energy efficiency.

- **'Air-conditioning system'** is a combination of all components required to provide a form of air treatment, in which temperature is controlled or can be lowered, possibly in combination with control of ventilation, humidity and air cleanliness.

- **'Boiler'** is the combined boiler body and burner-unit designed to transmit to water the heat released from combustion.

- **'Effective rated output'** (expressed in kW) is the maximum calorific output specified and guaranteed by the manufacturer as being deliverable, during continuous operation while complying with the useful efficiency indicated by the manufacturer.

- **'Heat pump'** is defined as a device or installation that extracts heat at low temperature from air, water or earth, and supplies the heat to the building.

A schedule or annex to the Directive sets out the general framework for the calculation of energy performance of buildings. Single-family houses of different types and apartment blocks are specifically included.

Articles 5 and 6 of the Directive refer to the **'useful floor area'** of new and existing buildings and those with a floor area measurement of **'over 1,000 sq. metres.'** This probably refers to very large public and other such buildings, such as office blocks. The Directive gives discretion to Member States not to apply the requirements in respect of certain buildings such as buildings used for worship and for religious activities, stand-alone buildings with a total useful floor area of less than 50 sq. metres, and residential buildings which are intended to be used less than four months of the year.

Article 7 contains vital information regarding the energy performance certificate. It states that Member States shall ensure that when buildings are constructed, sold or rented out, an energy performance certificate is made available to the owner or by the owner to the prospective buyer or tenant, as the case may be. The certificate is valid for a maximum of 10 years. Certification for apartments or units designed for separate use in blocks may be based on a common certification of the whole building for blocks with a common heating system, or on the assessment of another representative apartment in the same block.

EU MORTGAGES

Another recent development, which may impact on the purchase of homes and apartments in Ireland and other Member States, is a proposal by the European Commission to integrate the mortgage market throughout the European Union.

Coincidentally, this proposal is within the province of the former Minister for Finance, Mr Charlie McCreevy, who is the Single Market Commissioner.

The **EU Forum Group on Mortgage Credit**, established by the Commission in 2003, has proposed 48 legislative and non-legislative measures to boost the integration of the EU home loan market. Consumer protection, client credit assessment, mortgage brokers, registration systems, the law covering cross-border contracts and the financing of mortgages through capital markets have received attention in the various proposals put forward for consideration by the Commission.

Another EU study has revealed that only 1% of Europeans, who were mostly second-home owners or those in border regions, obtained mortgages from another country. The difficulty of comparing products, language and legal barriers, including differences in national provisions on consumer protection, such as early repayment rules, were given as reasons for this low take-up figure.

The Forum Group concluded that:

- EU legislation should bring into line national rules on early repayment fees and on calculating real interest rates.

- Information-sharing in credit databases and land registration systems (see E-Conveyancing below) should be encouraged by the Commission.

- There should be a deeper and more liquid secondary market for mortgage funding.

- Confusion over which national law applied to contracts when more than one country was involved could discourage cross-border mortgage transactions.

E-CONVEYANCING

Electronic technology, which speeds up considerably and renders more efficient the very many services that the public and their various agents have access to, is one of the great strides forward by society. The ability to log onto the Revenue website and perform a transaction, or onto your bank's website to do a money transfer, to pay a telephone bill or order groceries without leaving home, to complete a claim form in order to institute court proceedings - these are just a few of the **paperless transactions** that are possible as a result of technological innovation in recent years. If such technology could be applied to conveyancing, it would border on a revolution and result in a more expeditious and transparent process to the mutual benefit of practitioners and public alike, especially to house buyers.

A recent very comprehensive article on this subject in the Law Society's *Gazette* gave a progress up-date from other countries in the process of introducing an e-conveyancing system, including England and Wales, Scotland and New Zealand. It quoted part of the English Land Registry's 2004 Strategy for the implementation of e-conveyancing in England and Wales, stating that the essence of e-conveyancing was 'easier conveyancing for all,' resulting in reduced delays, cost savings, greater transparency and certainty, and reduced anxiety for those buying and selling property. In its vision of a paperless transaction model, the strategy stated:

"All communication between practitioners, lenders, Land Registry and other organisations involved in the conveyancing process will be capable of being electronic, as will all exchanges of formal documentation. Electronic communication between the professionals and the buyers and sellers may also be the norm. But it may not be possible to abolish paper totally. Some people, for example, may not be connected to the internet and communication using paper and the post will continue to be needed."

LAND REGISTRY

The Law Reform Commission has been laying the groundwork for the introduction of e-conveyancing in this country for the past two years. However, part and parcel with its introduction will be the need to carry out a root and branch reform of the antiquated Irish land and conveyancing law as well as introducing major procedural reforms. In this task the Commission has been working since Summer 2004, with the Department of Justice, Equality and Law Reform to update and modernise this country's conveyancing law. The Commission produced a consultation paper on the reform and modernisation of Irish land and conveyancing law in late 2004, as a prelude to the consultation process that it normally embarks on after publishing a consultation paper. In a previous chapter we saw how conveyancers are now able to access registration information on-line in the Land Registry, which is the overall winner of the eGovernment Awards 2005. This has simplified and speeded up the work of conveyancers and legal searchers in the Land Registry which had 769,000-paid transactions in 2004. It had more than 3,300 transactions conducted in this fashion each day through its electronic access service Four-fifths of the Land Registry's business is now conducted online.

Chapter 12

CLOSING ISSUES FOR EVERYBODY

As the time for the closing or completion of the transaction approaches in the case of the purchase of a **new** property, arrangements should be made to have a snag list drawn up and presented to the builder, either directly or through the solicitor acting for the buyer. The inspection should be carried out by an architect, engineer, building surveyor or other expert who has the expertise to identify a whole range of problems which, if left unattended at this stage, could lead to further difficulties after the buyer goes into possession. After the purchase money is paid over in full at the closing, the builder may become difficult to contact, leading to severe frustration and anger. Therefore, the time to establish if doors fail to close properly, if plasterwork is unfinished or badly finished or if there are problems in the plumbing or electrical systems, is before the closing, not after. The electricity, the water and the gas, if provided, should all be in working order to enable proper checks to be carried out. A crack in a wall has the potential to be much more serious than mere settlement and must be fully investigated by an expert as early as possible.

However, the mere fact that the buyer or his or her solicitor presents a snag list to the vendor does not mean that every item on the list will be taken care of. The builder or, most likely, the sub-contractors responsible for particular problems identified by the buyer, may tackle the problems on the snag list, but fail to deal with them at all or else did not do so adequately. Therefore, buyers should be prepared to re-check the house or apartment not once, but several times, before the closing to ensure that everything has been taken care of to their satisfaction. Very often a buyer will personally establish a good rapport with the site foreman. This may very beneficial for the buyer in getting things done.

In the case of **second-hand houses**, the buyer's expert will have surveyed the property much earlier, before the contract was signed. However, the buyer should not hesitate to visit the property on more than one occasion before closing. In this regard there is a condition in the **General Conditions of Sale**, which states that:

> 'the vendor shall accede to all such requests as may be made by the Purchaser for the inspection on a reasonable number of occasions and at reasonable times of the subject property (and the purchased chattels).'

Meanwhile, behind the scenes, the respective solicitors for the buyer and seller will have been working on such detail as raising and responding to the requisitions on the title and drafting the purchase deed. The purchaser's solicitor, in addition, will be drafting documents for the lending institution being used by the purchaser to provide the mortgage as well as making sure that anything that requires to be done by the lender will be completed then, rather than later in order to avoid the possibility of delaying the closing. Any **tax** issues arising on the sale or purchase will also be taken care of in the period leading up to the closing. It is not uncommon for some issue to arise following receipt of the vendor's replies to the requisitions sent out by the purchaser's solicitor. This might be a **planning** issue, for example, and the buyer's solicitor may require further information than was furnished in a stock answer by the seller's solicitor.

PARTNERS
In the lead up to the purchase, and certainly to the closing, an issue that will arise in some circumstances is the status in law of the person or persons buying the house or apartment. A purchase by an individual, or by a man and

woman legally married to each other in the eyes of the law, should be a straightforward transaction. However, the **2002 Census** revealed that there were **70,000 couples cohabiting** in this country. Three years on and it would be reasonable to believe that that number has increased considerably. They represent a sizeable portion of the population living together, so much so that the Law Reform Commission last year published a consultation paper concerning them entitled: *Cohabitees, Rights and Duties*. It dealt with such diverse topics as maintenance, succession, social welfare, pensions, tax, health, succession and **property.**

Any person who is thinking or planning to buy a house or apartment in **partnership** must have their legal position explained to them by their solicitor before they enter into a legally binding contract. A very experienced conveyancing solicitor, **Mr Paul O'Brien,** of **Smyth O'Brien Hegarty Solicitors**, Lower Abbey Street, Dublin, put together the following list of items that must be covered by such an agreement:

(1) Who the joint tenants are and what financial contribution they each made towards the purchase of the property?

(2) How long the agreement should last for?

(3) What happens if one of the parties dies or wants to realise his/her share of the house or apartment: should the other parties have first option to buy or should the property be sold and the proceeds divided?

(4) What arbitration mechanism should be used to evaluate the property in the event of someone leaving?

(5) Does a partner have the right to sublet and must that person meet with the approval of the other parties?

(6) Can one of the partners to the agreement take in a boyfriend/girlfriend?

These are very important questions that must be addressed by the partners, individually and collectively. Other questions which the partners should carefully consider should include the arrangements that should take place if one of them decides at a future date to leave and sell their interest, regarding the financial contributions they will each make towards repayment of the mortgage, insurance, other outgoings and, generally, towards the maintenance of the house or apartment. In the case of an apartment, there is the ever-increasing cost of the maintenance contract to be addressed.

It is vitally important that the two types of co-ownership are understood and discussed with the parties themselves. They should be advised as to the distinction between the two types, i.e., as joint tenants or as tenants in common. Therefore, where the conveyance is made to more than one grantee, it must be specified exactly how they are to take the property. In the case of a conveyance to a husband and wife, the fact that they own the property as joint tenants means that in the even of the death of one of them, the surviving spouse succeeds automatically to the other spouse's interest in the property. In the case of both a joint tenancy and a tenancy in common, the property held by the persons concerned is held by them concurrently, so that as far as third parties are concerned, the co-owners of the property must be treated as a single unit. However, with regard to themselves individually, the positions of co-owners holding under a joint tenancy and those holding under a tenancy in common are very different. It is extremely important that this is understood by people buying as partners.

JOINT TENANTS

What exactly does this term mean? It means that each owns all and yet owns nothing - one cannot sell his or her share without the consent of the other because they do not own a share of the property as such. As we have just seen in the case of a husband and wife, people who own as joint tenants enjoy a **right of survivorship** - if one party dies, the other succeeds to that party's interest in the property automatically. Another example of this is where a couple share a joint deposit account in a bank or building society. If one dies, the other is entitled to the total proceeds of the account. Right of survivorship is the central principle of a joint tenancy, according to Wylie's *Irish Land Law*. Because of this right, neither of them can make a will and leave his or her share in the property to somebody other than to the other co-tenant.

As we referred to above, the Law Reform Commission's Consultation Paper deals with several topics regarding couples cohabiting who would not, as the law stands, enjoy the same rights as husbands and wives, e.g. fiscal rights. Under section 14 of the **Family Home Protection Act 1976**, a conveyance of a family home to the spouses as joint tenants is exempt from stamp duty. It is also exempt from land registration fees, Registry of Deed's fees or court fees, where the home was immediately prior to this particular transaction owned by either spouse or both of them otherwise as joint tenants. A practical example of this occurred when, as a law student in the early 1980s, it gave this author great satisfaction to transfer the home of his parents from the sole name of his father into the joint names of both parents and to have the transfer document stamped '**exempt from stamp duty**' by the Revenue Office in Dublin Castle. More important, it gave each parent an easy mind that in the event of the death of either, the home would automatically become sole owner by right of survivorship.

TENANTS IN COMMON
There is no right of survivorship in a tenancy in common. A tenant in common has a distinct and separate interest or share in the property from the date that the tenancy in common began. If two people buy a property as tenants

in common, they each hold a **separate share.** In the case of a conveyance to co-owners as tenants in common, their precise shares in the property should be specified.

ADVICE

Because of the foregoing, partners buying a house or apartment as partners are advised that it is in their best interests individually to purchase as 'tenants in common.' If the property is held jointly when such a relationship breaks down and each of the partners go their separate way, it can lead to severe difficulties, such as trying to establish how much each of them should receive from a sale of the property, especially if they had made unequal contributions towards the purchase, and subsequent payment of the mortgage and maintenance of the property.

Some cohabiting couples agree to sell the property and simply divide the proceeds, if any, after the mortgage and other charges are discharged. But other relationships do not break up in such agreement, especially where they contributed unequal amounts towards the purchase and maintenance of the property. Most of this trouble can be avoided by the partners entering a contract to purchase the property as tenants in common. If they want to make sure that their share in the house or apartment passes to the other on their own death, they should **make a will** setting out their intentions to that effect. In that way, they will ensure that their respective share does not pass outside their union to another family member as next-of-kin. If they are adamant that they wish each other's share to pass to the other automatically on death and advise the solicitor of this, then the solicitor will act as advised and ensure that the couple buy as joint tenants.

THE BIG DAY

The day that a person or persons get ownership of their own home is like no other. In the build up to it, there can be worry and concern right up to the end and the relief that comes with the hand-over of the keys can seem like an anti-climax if the process had been difficult but, if it ran smoothly as most do, it is a wonderful feeling of satisfaction. At last a place of your own, a place to call home!

In respect of a new house, the closing date is normally the completion date of the house as set out in the building agreement. The closing may take place in the offices of the seller or vendor's solicitor. Usually so little is seen to happen at this simple ceremony that the purchaser may wonder what all the fuss was about. In reality, the solicitors for both parties will have done most of the work long before this day dawns. The solicitor for the purchaser will have drafted the necessary documents and, in fact, will have had the purchaser sign them a number of weeks before the closing. The deed of transfer or conveyance through which the title is transferred from the seller to the buyer will be signed at the closing.

On that date the purchaser, through his solicitor, will hand over the balance of the purchase money due. Title will then pass to the purchaser and the keys are handed to the purchaser in an informal way, with handshakes and congratulations being offered to the new owner that is if the purchaser is present. They may not be and do not need to be, once the solicitor has the necessary authority. This is sometimes expressed in a formal **Power of Attorney** document (see Glossary of Terms) to act on behalf of the purchaser, or vendor, as the case may be, but especially for the purchaser, which will have been signed well in advance of the closing to enable the solicitors to complete certain transactions.

There are many documents that the purchaser's solicitor will require at the closing. They will vary as between completion documents for registered land and unregistered land. This is an area that client need not be concerned with as the solicitors will be checking documents of title as specified in the contract.

LAST MINUTE SEARCHES

Searches against the property will also be carried out right up to the last minute before completion. This is to safeguard the purchaser's interest in making certain that there were no late charges registered against the property. If, in fact, there was, and the purchaser was unaware of it, they would be deemed to have had notice of the charge and to have purchased the property with the charge. The consequences of this happening could be extremely damaging, not only to the purchaser but also to the solicitor who could be held to be professionally negligent in not carrying out a late search.

The solicitor for the purchaser will also ensure that the requisitions on title, which had been raised, are fully answered and complied with. It is only when the solicitor has ensured that everything is in order and that the purchaser is getting a good marketable title, free from any encumbrances that he or she will allow the title to be transferred to the purchaser. The solicitor will already have ordered or carried out last minute checks to ensure there were no late charges registered against the property. A check will also be carried out to make sure there are no outstanding bills for electricity, gas, and telephone or refuse services. The seller must pay all such bills before a sale is completed.

AN IMPORTANT LAST DUTY FOR THE PURCHASER

At this very late stage and just before the actual transfer of title, it may be advisable for the purchaser to have a last-minute look around the property. This would usually only apply to second-hand properties. The main reason why this may be necessary is to see if any chattels were to be included after negotiation as part of the sale or, perhaps, as part of a separate agreement, are still in the property. Obviously, it will not always be possible to gain entry at the 11th hour, as the vendor will have moved out in anticipation of the imminent closing. In that event, the vendor's solicitor or estate agent, who may still have the keys to the property, should be contacted by the purchaser's solicitor to facilitate the purchaser. This is a reasonable request and would be covered by the condition in the contract that allows for reasonable inspection.

To the author's certain knowledge, the purchasers of a large detached house in the suburbs of a mid-west city in the USA could not wait to see their new home after the closing in the attorney's office. But they were aghast to find that the white, timber fencing that had run right around the extensive property was no longer in place. It had been uprooted and taken by the seller, when vacating the property. It is not unusual for purchasers to find after the completion that fixtures and fittings, which may have been the subject of an informal verbal agreement, have been removed. This could happen because of genuine forgetfulness on the part of the seller or even deliberately by a seller who had second thoughts about including some item in the sale price, despite having agreed personally with the potential buyer during an early viewing.

According to *Wylie*, the law relating to fixtures is 'a rather technical area, involving general principles by no means always easy to apply to specific cases' and the best advice for both seller and buyer, who are agreed that certain items should be included in the purchase, should be formally set down in writing, if necessary by including a list in the particulars of the contract or scheduling it to the contract itself. In that situation, there can be no room for confusion, 'loss of memory' or second thoughts.

GLOSSARY OF TERMS

Adjustable Rate –An interest rate that changes periodically in relation to an index, which will result in payments increasing or decreasing accordingly.

Agent – A person who represents a seller of property, a buyer of property or both.

Annual percentage rate – The cost of credit on a yearly basis, expressed as a percentage. It reflects the true cost of repaying a loan, such as a mortgage, as it includes the up-front costs paid to obtain the loan. It does not include mortgage insurance and other such costs independent of the mortgage.

Annuity mortgage – A standard capital and interest repayment mortgage.

Application fee – The fee charged by a lending institution for an individual to apply for a mortgage. It may include a fee for a valuation or appraisal of the property being purchased.

Appraisal – A fee charged by an appraiser to provide an opinion of market value as of a specific date. Another term for 'valuation.'

Balloon payment – A lump sum payment for the unpaid balance of a loan, payable at the end of repayment period.

Buyer's agent – An estate agent who has made an agreement to represents the interests of the buyer exclusively in return for a fee, represented usually by a percentage of the price achieved for the property.

Cap – The maximum allowable allowance, for either payment or interest rate, for a specified period of time on an adjustable rate mortgage.

Certificate of compliance – A certificate furnished by an architect or engineer, but usually the former, showing that a property has been built in accordance with the planning permission granted for that property.

Charge – A charge or mortgage registered against a property.

Conveyancing – The practical legal work involved in transferring legal ownership of property.

Closing – The completion of a sale or purchase of real property.

Contract of sale – The written agreement between the buyer and seller of a property containing such information as the names of the parties, a full description of the property, the price, terms and conditions.

Covenant (restrictive) – A condition in a contract restricting a party to the contract in some manner.

Deed of trust – An agreement used to pledge a home or other real estate as security for a loan.

Deed of conveyance or transfer – The document used to execute a transfer of the legal title in property from one party to another.

Deed of assignment – The document used to execute a transfer of the interest in a leased property from one party to another.

Down payment (deposit) – The difference between the purchase price and that portion of the purchase price being financed by a mortgage from the lender. Most lenders require the down payment to be paid from the buyer's own funds.

Encumbrance – A claim against a property by a third party which usually affects the ability to transfer ownership of the property.

Equity – The difference between the value of a property and the total of any outstanding mortgage or loan against it.

Fee simple – The highest estate that can be conveyed. It entitles the owner to the entire property so that he or she can dispose of it unconditionally during their lifetime.

First mortgage – A mortgage which is in first lien position, taking priority over all other liens (which are financial encumbrances) on the property.

Fixture – Personal chattels attached to property which may be severed and removed by the party who has affixed them, i.e., the owner. As a general rule fixtures once annexed to the freehold become part of the realty. The controlling question in determining whether fixtures are part of the realty or not is whether they are permanently fixed or not. Generally speaking, anything which is intended to make a permanent improvement to the property and is affixed and cannot be removed without damaging the structure, such as a bath or mantelpiece, is a fixture and belongs to the property. In contrast, anything of a movable character, such as an electric light fitting, items of furniture and carpet, is a 'fitting' and generally would not belong to the property.

Fixed rate – A mortgage interest rate which is fixed for a period of the loan repayment.

Folio – The file or record of ownership of land which is registered in the Land Registry.

Foreclosure – This is the word used to describe the process under which a lender recovers a property from a defaulting borrower and re-sells it.

House insurance – A compulsory contract of insurance that the borrower must take out to insure against the risk of damage being caused to the building itself by fire or other identified causes.

Land certificate – Often referred to as 'the land cert' it is evidence of ownership of property registered in the Land Registry.

Land Registry – The State institution where lands are registered. They are at three locations, two in Dublin and one in Waterford. One is situated at Block 1, Irish Life Centre, Lower Abbey Street, Dublin 1 (tel. 01-6707500; Lo-Call 1890-333001) for counties Kildare and Wicklow; a second is at Setanta Centre, Nassau Street, Dublin 2 (same tel. numbers as above) covering counties Dublin and those west of the River Shannon and the third is located at New Government Buildings, Cork Road, Waterford for counties Cork, Kerry, Limerick, Waterford, Carlow, Kilkenny, Wexford, Laois, Offaly and Tipperary (tel. 051-30300 and Lo-Call 1890 333002).

Lien – A legal claim against a property or part of a property that acts as a bar on the property being disposed of until the owner of the lien is paid off, e.g. a solicitor's lien in respect of outstanding fees.

Loan offer – The letter in which the lender offers a mortgage to a borrower and the terms and conditions of repayment.

Mortgage – A loan given by a lender to a borrower towards the purchase of real property. Legally, it utilises real estate as security or collateral to provide for repayment, should the borrower default on the terms of the loan. If the latter happens, the lender or mortgagee may sell the property to recoup the amount of money loaned.

Mortgagee: The lender in a mortgage loan transaction.

Mortgagor - The borrower in a mortgage loan transaction.

Mortgage broker – Takes loan applications and processes the necessary documentation for the lender on behalf of a borrower.

Mortgage insurance – Insurance purchased by the borrower to insure the lender in the event of the borrower defaulting. It is compulsory for the borrower to buy such insurance as a condition of getting a mortgage loan.

Mortgage payment protection – A policy of insurance that a mortgagor *may* take out to afford protection in the event of illness or redundancy under which the insurer will pay the mortgage for a period of up to a maximum of 12 months.

Registry of Deeds – The registry where legal documents usually affecting land are registered. It is situated in Henrietta Street, Dublin 1 (tel. 01-6707500).

Root of title – The principal legal document on which the chain of title is rooted or commences.

Searches – This is what it says, a search to establish if the vendor has a legal right to sell the property and, in addition, to ascertain if there is any charge or interest registered against the property.

Structural survey – A thorough inspection of a property by a suitably qualified person to establish if the fabric and structure are sound. It is usually ordered by the potential buyer in advance of entering into a contract to purchase the property. It is most suitable for older, second-hand homes. It can also include specialist reports on particular features such as roofing, damp proofing and foundations.

Valuation – A survey or inspection of a property carried out by a qualified surveyor to establish of it provides good security for the loan or mortgage, i.e. whether it is a good investment.

Variable rate – An interest rate that changes from time to time in relation to an index. Payments may increase or decrease accordingly.

USEFUL WEBSITE ADDRESSES

www.askaboutmoney.ie
www.daft.ie
www.independentdirectory.ie
www.lawsociety.ie
www.myhome.ie
www.nicemove.ie
www.realestate.ie
www.revenue.ie

INDEX

LOCATION - ✓

PHANTOM BIDDERS.
  PRIVATE TREATY

Seal BID.

LAW of CONTRACT

STATE AGENCY 2% on selling price.

WWW PROPERTY game 1.e.